Going Nowhere Slow

Autumn into Winter

David Muir

For

Lynn, Kirsten and Rebecca

Cover background

Image of autumn leaves by S_Bachstroem.

Going Nowhere Slow: Autumn into Winter

Contents

Appendices

Preview

Introduction

This book, *Going Nowhere Slow: Autumn into Winter* is the first book in the *Going Nowhere Slow* trilogy, and it covers August 17th to December 31st, 2015.

The other books in the *Going Nowhere Slow* trilogy are:

Going Nowhere Slow: Winter into Spring, which covers January 1st to April 29th, 2016.

Going Nowhere Slow: Spring into Summer, which covers May 1st to August 17th, 2016.

A Brief Background

In the past, I was going nowhere fast, and now I'm going nowhere slow.

How did that come to pass? Read on if you want to know.

1955 was a good year.

Jim Henson invents Kermit the Frog, West Germany becomes a sovereign nation, Rosa Parks refuses to obey a bus driver in Montgomery, Alabama and Cardiff is declared capital of Wales.

September 18th was particularly special.

The United Kingdom annexes Rockall, the People newspaper announces that Guy Burgess and Donald Maclean were spies and not diplomats as had been previously reported and, I was born. I was the fourth of five siblings with two older sisters, a younger sister and an older brother. I was brought up in the Scottish Borders town of Selkirk.

As a child, I liked watching things, I liked growing things and I loved burning things, in bonfires, with matches, or with a magnifying glass. Was I genetically predisposed to become a chemistry teacher (or perhaps an arsonist), or did my early environment and experience lead me towards it? Probably a bit of both.

After primary school, I went to the local Selkirk High School before heading off to St Andrews University in 1973 where I did a bit of physics and geology, but chemistry was most fun so that's what I concentrated on. Coming from a small town like Selkirk, I enjoyed St Andrews as it was only around twice the size of Selkirk. You were less likely to get lost, in more ways than one, than if you went to college or university in a larger place like Edinburgh. There was more to St Andrews than just the academic and tourist attributes: I met my wife Lynn there, in 1974.

After St Andrews, I spent a year at Moray House College of Education in Edinburgh, qualifying as a chemistry and science teacher. My first school placement as a student teacher was at Selkirk High School, much to the discombobulation of some of my old teachers. 'Poacher-turned-gamekeeper' was one of the more delicate expressions used to describe me; this was taken as a complement.

Lynn and I moved to Edinburgh where she worked for one of the large financial institutions and I taught in Holy Rood High School for five years, moving to Portobello High School for the next thirty two years, before retiring from teaching. This brings me to why I'm actually writing this document.

When colleagues found out that I was retiring, the question most commonly asked was how I would fill in my time. I found this rather difficult to understand because as far as I was concerned, there is not enough time in the day to do all the things that I want to do. My trouble is that I'm curious. I want to know the how's and why's of stuff, not just the stuff itself. A thing I found slightly sad was that ex-colleagues who had retired before me were asking me the same question as to how I would fill my day.

I didn't really want to answer birds, insects, flowers, trees, mosses, fungi, how they interact and affect each other, the chemistry and chemicals in their different constituent parts, how they evolved and continue to evolve their mechanisms to attract and defend, and the etymology of how they all got their common and scientific names.

I didn't really want to answer clouds, their formation and nomenclature, how they are beautiful in their own right, the optical effects they exhibit, the weather patterns associated with clouds; never mind astronomy, literature, history, gardening, writing and lots of other interests, pastimes and assorted ways of keeping fit or experiencing new environments, situations and learning.

So what did I answer? I'd generally say that I like wandering and pondering, and leave it at that. If I got some funny looks and comments, I'd expand this short answer with the explanation that I like watching stuff like the sky, and grass growing, and that I liked thinking. Folk would then smile and nod, then walk off shaking their head, probably assuming that I'd already entered my dotage. Maybe they were right.

It crossed my mind that perhaps I should document how I kept myself entertained during my first year of retirement, if I survived it, given that Lynn may get a little annoyed with me underfoot, metaphorically speaking. Not a diary of daily events, but a log of what entertains me, and of some the ponderings around the science that underlie the simple things that we see, experience and take for granted, and how knowledge of that science raises the simple and mundane to remarkable and marvellous.

Writing *Going Nowhere Slow* has been one of my ways of staying sane and entertaining myself at the same time. If anyone reads this and finds it diverting, informative, and perhaps amusing or thought-provoking in parts, then that makes the writing of *Going Nowhere Slow* even more worthwhile. The writing has been fun and satisfying in itself.

I have included appendices of some of the fungi, plants and animals which you'll meet in these three books. There are also appendices of some of the websites, books and beers which have enhanced my life during my wanderings and ponderings through my first year of retirement.

August

'The chief beauty about time

is that you cannot waste it in advance.

The next year, the next day, the next hour are lying ready for you,

as perfect, as unspoiled,

as if you had never wasted or misapplied

a single moment in all your life.

You can turn over a new leaf every hour

if you choose.'

Arnold Bennett (1886-1931)

'Much as we may wish to make a new beginning, some part of us resists doing so as though we were making the first step toward disaster.'

William Throsby Bridges (1861-1915)

'It does not matter how slowly you go, as long as you do not stop.'

Confucius (551-471 BCE)

August 17th

Sisyphus finally succeeds.

Sisyphus was king of Ephyra, now known as Corinth, and he was not a nice person. In fact, he was most unpleasant, a nasty piece of mythological work. But worst, he gave away one of Zeus's secrets for which he was well and truly punished. Sisyphus was made, for all eternity, to push a huge, round rock up a hill and, just as it got to the top, the rock would roll back down and he had to start pushing it up all over again. Sisyphean is the adjective that describes a never-ending, repetitive task.

So where does my Sisyphean success come from? Today is my first day of retirement from teaching, after thirty seven years of toil.

The 15th August, 1978, was my first day of paid teaching. For thirty seven years, on a day sometime in the middle of August every year, I'd put my shoulder to the Sisyphean rock and start pushing uphill. Some years more than others, a greater effort was required to keep the rock moving onwards and upwards and not roll back and flatten me. Granted, as some of you may be thinking, teachers get reasonable breaks at Christmas and Easter, enough to stop and draw breath: but that rock was only ever temporarily held in place.

The spring term in school was, once upon a time, supposed to be less onerous. The slope the rock was pushed up was less steep and the top of the hill did not seem so far away. The hill's summit was usually conquered in the last week in June, when the school's academic year came to a close. The rock rolled back down the hill ready for the coming August, but unlike Sisyphus, teachers have the respite of the summer holiday. July and August are two important reasons for entering the teaching profession.

July is easily enjoyed, as is the first week in August, but as the ides of August approach, the ominous threat of the Sisyphean rock increases

10

until, once again, the sinews strain as your back bends to the task of pushing the rock up the slope. At this time of year, the following June seems a distant dream: but not for me.

Today is my first official day of retirement, and the first day of the rest of my life.

August 20th

I live in an old house, in the Grange area of Edinburgh, built around 1860. It has a large garden, about a third of an acre, and is surrounded by a stone wall two metres high. The wall protects from winds and can act as a sun trap. No matter the time of day, if the sun is in the sky, there is a bit of wall facing it. This begs for a seat to be positioned there, with me in it, especially if any wind is coming from the direction behind the wall against which the sun is shining.

A lot of time is spent in the garden but not too much gardening is done. I like thinking about what needs done and then procrastinating, but luckily, procrastination can always be put off until another day. I also read a lot in the garden, which I treat much like some people may use a conservatory, if they are lucky enough to have one. Seats are situated in the best sun-traps round the garden so, as the sun crosses the sky, I cross the grass to a sunnier seat to avoid being in the shade.

August 21st

I was sitting in what I call the morning seat. It faces roughly east and catches the post-breakfast sun; the Scotsman crossword was being particularly cryptic so I was a little frustrated.

Then I was downright irritated. Sometimes the reproductive imperative really annoys me. Not my own, but that of other animals which frequent my own little Arcadia. These beasts can conspire to spoil the satisfaction that I derive from growing my own fruit and vegetables.

Brussels sprouts are a food for which I've not had to develop a taste. I've always liked them, but best straight from the stem and into the steamer. This is not just the tastiest way to eat them, but the healthiest. Brussels sprouts belong to *Brassica oleracea*, the name which covers broccoli, cabbage, kale and the like. Think of the Brussels sprout plant as a tall cabbage which doesn't develop the big cabbage heart but lots of small cabbages next to where leaf stalks meets the main stem. These small cabbages are the sprouts, the sideshoots of the plant.

Two years ago, cabbage root fly, *Delia radicum,* devastated my brassicas and me. The fly lays its eggs on the soil close to a brassica plant, the eggs hatch, the larvae head for the roots then munch away underground, unseen and certainly unloved. To counter *Delia's* destruction, last year, I kept my young plantlets in a cold frame so the fly couldn't get near them. When I planted them out, I dressed the plantlet stems with little cardboard collars at soil-surface level, so the little *Delias* failed to get close enough to the soil next to the main stem to make egg-laying worthwhile.

The sprout plants didn't go straight into garden soil but into large holes filled with multipurpose compost, the stuff you buy three bags for a tenner at the garden centre. This is to avoid clubroot, a common disease of brassicas. Clubroot spores can survive in soil for years, hence the multipurpose compost, which gives the sprouts a cleaner environment to commence healthy growth.

Is this good garden practice or am I getting paranoiac? Perhaps paranoia is required for good gardening, given that many chemicals which were once used to protect plants from pests and pathogens have now been removed from the garden centre shelves, for good environmental and health reasons.

Last year, these precautions were taken and sturdy, attractive plants grew. It wasn't only me who found the plants attractive; so did the local wood pigeons which pecked the plants to literally bits. I'd thought a few days without a pigeon defence system wouldn't be much of a risk but, how wrong. A protective, plastic mesh was quickly erected in the hope that the mutilated Brussels sprouts plants might recover. They did and I drew much satisfaction from this because in netting the sprouts, I'd also defended the plants from the next, predicted scourge, the cabbage white butterfly.

The cabbage white butterfly, *Pieris brassicae,* likes to lay its pale yellow eggs on, unsurprisingly, brassicas, usually on the underside of leaves. This affords the eggs and hatching larvae some protection from predators, mainly birds, but some insects and spiders will also attack eggs and larvae. The cabbage white has a wingspan of around 5cm so my 2cm square, plastic mesh would be just the job to keep the butterflies from my sprout plants.

When you least expect it, hubris jumps up and bites you on the bum. Hubris is that quality of over-confidence as you're flying high, but results in a sudden crash-land on the road to reality. What clipped my wings? Reproductive imperative! That of the cabbage white butterflies which were flitting about above my beloved Brussels sprouts *inside* my prophylactic, plastic mesh. Note the plural, butterflies, not the singular, butterfly.

Rather than rashly put on the judge's black cap when sentencing perpetrators to death, I put on my thinking hat. I sat and watched the insects to see if I could detect how they got into the plastic cage. The butterflies landed on the inside of the plastic mesh, proceeded to fold up their wings and morph their body shape, like a kid's transformer toy, and squeeze out through the gap. I watched them exit and then again enter in the same manner.

This was last year and I spent the tail-end of the summer frequently picking green caterpillars from the heads of the sprout plants where the most tender leaves and the best hidey-holes are to be found. The damaged leaves grew on to resemble Emmental cheese, but I did have the pleasure of throwing the still-living caterpillars on to the grass, much to the delight of one of the local robins. This was last year so let me bring you up to date.

This year, I've used the same strong plastic to keep out the pigeons, and a light, finer 1.5cm mesh netting to stymie the cabbage whites. With a smug smile, I watched frustrated cabbage white butterflies flutter above and around this plastic fortress. The plants had been so well shielded that this year they were thriving, so much so, that some of their leaves were even pushing up and outwards against the protective net.

The smug smile was swiftly wiped from my face when I saw a butterfly alight on the plastic surround, shove its rear-end through the mesh. It struggled to position its ovipositor, its egg-laying apparatus at the end of its abdomen, on to a leaf at least 2cm below the mesh. The butterfly was hunched over and straining, rather like a small, constipated child on the toilet. It was attempting to lay an egg on the Brussels sprout leaf. From my point of view, it was sadly successful, but from the butterfly's perspective, its reproductive imperative won the day.

You must take what you can from your defeats so over the next few days, I'll follow the development of the five little, yellow eggs which were found a centimetre or two beneath the mesh. This is free entertainment. Take that, hubris.

As well as being a good source of vitamins C and K, and a reasonable source of B vitamins, sprouts contain sulforaphane which could well have anticancer properties. Some of these chemicals are lost when sprouts are boiled, but less so when the sprouts are steamed. Clinical trials are also being conducted with sulforaphane as a treatment for autism spectrum disorder.

There is a down side to sulforaphane. It's a compound that contains sulfur so it causes your flatulence to be a little unpleasant for those in your immediate vicinity, a small price for your friends and acquaintances to pay for your gains in long-term health.

August 23rd

I rescued a pallet today. It was alone and unwanted, situated between two of the large communal waste-bins which are a common sight these days along Edinburgh's highways and byways. Such bins were introduced to prevent rubbish from blowing about the capital's streets. Before their introduction, citizens' rubbish was left on pavements at the roadside in plastic, usually black, bin-bags. The local wildlife would rip these apart in an orgy of destruction and subsequent feasting, leaving the streets strewn with assorted, inedible detritus. The cessation of bin-bag use has caused a concomitant reduction in the number of city foxes which could previously be seen wandering the leafy suburbs of the city's south side where I live. At almost any time of day, one of these cocky animals could pass you on the pavement with a supercilious look as if you are intruding on its territory, which I suppose you are.

The decline in urban foxes was, in some ways, sad, but the streets are much tidier on rubbish-collection days especially when the wind is up. Foxes were certainly not the only culprits in bin-bag destruction: seagulls were probably the greater nuisance.

I have often benefitted from picking up material by large waste-bins. Whereas people would previously only put out rubbish of a size similar to bin-bags, it now appears to be acceptable to leave large refuse items, such as mattresses and furniture. In past times, these would have been left out for free special uplift, but in these modern days of austerity, local councils demand payment for special uplifts so it is no surprise that bulky junk is left by the large, communal bins.

Unintended consequences are unpredicted by local authorities when new schemes are introduced, but sometimes lucky passers-by like me can be the beneficiary. The pallet which I rescued today was not too dirty and was solidly constructed: but it was in need of a new home and owner. The north side of my house is a pallet sanctuary.

There are donkey sanctuaries, horse sanctuaries, cat sanctuaries and dog sanctuaries for animals which are no longer needed nor loved by their former owners. So, why not have a pallet sanctuary? I rescue pallets dumped on the street and give them a better future. A pallet is not just for Christmas; they need ownership all year round and they need to find new purpose after having been disparaged and abandoned.

Many kind people are willing to offer a home and give new functionality to salvaged pallets. Whole pallets can be used to make large compost bins. I have three, directly adjacent to each other to ease compost aeration by turning the half-rotted material from one bin into a neighbouring empty bin. 'Makes good muck,' as my father would say.

Pallets can be dismantled. I use a re-homed crowbar, and the liberated timber can be put to good use strengthening compromised compost bins and enhancing the integrity of shoogly garden furniture: the wooden table by my siesta-seat was on its literal last legs until I applied appropriate re-enforcement of palletial origin.

The siesta-seat, in its current incarnation, comprises of spars of wood from an abandoned futon. I consider this as one way of integrating Eastern culture into my garden. This was not the first futon that I've rescued. The swing-bench at the bottom of the garden disintegrated a long time ago and the swing part was replaced completely by a restructured futon which had been discarded by its former owner(s). I'm only talking about the wooden parts of the forsaken futon. I had no use for the fold-up futon mattresses which were left by the bins where they were dumped.

As I sit of an evening on the swing-bench facing west, watching the cloud colours change as the sun sets, or when I snooze in the afternoon facing south on the siesta-seat, I sometimes wonder what sights these futon spars have seen. Well, not so much sights seen, as the futon would have been covered by a mattress, but more, sounds that it heard, or seismic movements that it experienced: perhaps the earth moved. The likelihood is that the straps of futon wood won't be hearing or feeling the same again. On a practical note, futon straps of wood are just long enough so that when you lie on a bench constructed of them, you don't feel too cramped and can stretch out in comfort. They're a bit springy, so a couple of cross-spars make things feel a little more secure.

Pallets, like donkeys, can be retired to a pleasant, countryside location where horses are not uncommon. My wife, Lynn, likes horses, but getting on to them can be a bit tricky. A much-appreciated birthday present was a mounting-block constructed from several pallets. It was about three feet by four feet at the base, with three steps up to be three-foot high; the steps were covered in chicken wire for good traction. The mounting-block was built next to the pallet sanctuary at the side of the house and stress-tested with my own fourteen stones as assurance against structural calamity, a necessary test as some stable-goers are amply proportioned.

To appreciate the versatility to which pre-loved pallets can be put, visit local allotments. Allotmenteers, or plotters as I like to call them, are experts at reusing pallets; gates, barriers, fences, raised beds, supports, edging, seating and tables are some of the possible uses. Pallet re-use is only limited by your imagination, or lack of it. There are wonderful websites which show how to make creative furniture from pallets and other recycled wood (www.homedit.com/21-ways-of-turning-pallets-into-unique-pieces-of-furniture).

From where is the word 'pallet' derived?

'Palus' is Latin for 'stake' or 'post', a rough piece of wood with a point which can be stuck in the ground, and this gives us the word 'pale' (now little used) for such a stick, and 'paling' fences made of 'pales'. Such a fence defined a safe area and 'beyond the pale' identifies areas outside that safe space. We also have 'palisade' for protection and 'impaling' for those who deserve it. A 'pallet' is made of rough bits of wood or stakes.

On the other hand, the Latin 'palea', for 'straw', gives us the French 'paille', then 'paillete' and 'pallet', a mattress of straw or a makeshift bed. A pallet is a crude bed on which cargo is transported. 'Palus' or 'palea'? Make your etymological choice, or perhaps even sleep on it.

Pallas Athena was the Greek goddess of wisdom, courage, inspiration, civilization, law and justice, mathematics, strength, war strategy, the arts and crafts; the most versatile of deities. Might I suggest that, given her multitude of talents, that Pallas Athena be proposed as the Guardian Goddess of pallets, which are indubitably the Swiss army knives of recyclable treasure?

August 25th

My south-facing siesta-seat has none of its original wood. Bits have rotted and been replaced on an ongoing basis, rather like what happens with our own bodies. Many of the cells in your body are not all the same ones as last week, never mind last year. After about eight or nine years we are essentially new people, other than some heart-muscle cells and cells from the lenses in your eyes which last, more or less, a lifetime. The turnover time for some types of cell in the gut is around four days, lung alveoli about eight days, skin epidermis from ten to thirty days and fat cells about eight years. No wonder I have problems shifting my spare tyre.

So I am lying on the siesta-seat, stretched out on a sunny, summer's day, languid. Sleep is toying with me, tempting me to succumb to her charms. I wavered within the magic moments between awareness and gentle descent into shallow slumber, but could hear short pops, like the sound of the electric spark when you press the electric lighter on your gas cooker. This brought me back to near wakefulness, but with eyes still closed, I tried to imagine what it could possibly be?

I ascertained that the sound was originating from over the wall next door, or more precisely, from above the wall next door. The source was a yellow-flowered shrub which reached a few feet above the wall and its seed pods were popping in the heat of the sun. It was a Common Broom, *Cytisus scoparius,* a botanical name that combines both Greek and Latin. The Greek, 'kytisos', meaning 'trefoil', which pertains to the leaves, and the Latin, 'scopa', a 'broom', a brush made of twigs tied to a stick. There's no prize for guessing what the historical, and probably pre-historical, use was for the Common Broom.

Broom has attributes which allow it to successfully colonise disturbed sites with poor soils. In many areas of the west coast of America, where forestry is a major industry, broom is viewed as an invasive species as it inhibits reforestation by competing with tree seedlings after timber has been harvested. Nitrogen is an essential nutrient for plant growth, and is a limiting factor in soils which have been impoverished by heavy cropping, as in forestry, but broom has attributes which circumvent this impediment to its growth.

Broom is a successful competitor because it is a legume, a plant that has the ability to capture, or 'fix', nitrogen from the air. It achieves this through a symbiotic relationship with rhizobium bacteria, living in nodules on the roots of the broom. Symbiosis is a relationship where two unrelated types of organism live together, usually to their mutual benefit; think of your own symbiotic relationship with the hundred trillion bacteria which live in your gut. Broom also has a deep tap root, an adaption which allows it to colonise relatively dry areas.

The broom's seed pods turn black in late summer, dry out and warp, which, on sunny days, results in an explosive separation of the two halves of the seedpod, dispersing the seeds with some speed and the characteristic piezo-electric pop. It's fun to poke leguminous seed pods which are ready to pop, or even better, to encourage some unsuspecting youngster to poke at seedpods stored on a sunny windowsill. Watch the child's reaction when they realise why you insisted on them wearing safety glasses. Mechanical, or ballistic, self-dispersal of seeds such as gorse and broom only removes the seeds a limited distance from the parent plant but this is no hindrance to the plant's success as is indicated by the swathes of broom and gorse on hillsides.

Both broom and gorse have evolved a secondary seed-dispersal mechanism through a further symbiosis, with ants. In The New Phytologist (March 27th, 1909), F.E. Weiss, Professor of Botany at the University of Manchester, published a paper entitled, *'The Dispersal of the Seeds of the Gorse and the Broom by Ants'*.

Professor Weiss observed that ants use existing paths and roadways to facilitate the transport of food to their nests, and that there was a rectilinear distribution of gorse bushes along roadsides and disused paths. He used this information to hypothesise that ants were the cause of straight lines of bushes in places where clumps, not lines, would normally have been expected.

To prove his hypothesis, Weiss conducted experiments by laying gorse seeds on ant highways to see if they would pick up the seeds and carry them along their straight tracks: they duly did. He concluded:

> 'We may therefore, I think, place the gorse and the broom in
> the category of plants, the seeds of which are dispersed by ants

in addition to the earlier dispersal within a nearer radius, by the explosive contraction of the ripe seed pod (autochory).'

Explaining:

'Ants are particularly attracted by the oil-containing caruncle, and as the experiments have shown, can and will carry the seeds of the gorse about.

The curious rectilinear distribution of gorse-bushes along actual or disused paths and roadways as illustrated by the instances on the Yorkshire Moor and the Derbyshire plateau does not seem explicable by ordinary dispersal due to the explosive dehiscence of the dry capsule, but can be paralleled by the distribution of such plants as the Celandine along the ant-runs.'

There are lots of interesting ways by which wind, water and animals are vectors involved in seed dispersal, but more of these later.

August 26th

I thought that I'd check on the health of the Brussels sprouts, the progress of the cabbage white butterfly eggs and the integrity of the plastic mesh coverings. As I was approaching the sprout bed, I saw that a small bird, which I took to be a dunnock, sometimes called a hedge sparrow, had got under the netting and was feeding unobtrusively, half-hidden by the sprouts' lower leaves. The bird wasn't a dunnock, but a wren and it was getting agitated as I drew near: then magic!

I bent to lift the bottom of the netting to give it a means of escape, when the wren flew straight at the mesh and passed right through it. I looked for a hole in the plastic net but there was none. I was flummoxed. The realisation struck that the wren must have escaped through one of the net squares, length of side only 1.5cm.

Animals which live in an environment where they may have to escape predators through tight spaces have evolved so that if their skull can get through a gap, the rest of their body can normally follow. A wren's skull is 1cm high by 1.3cm wide (www.skullsite.com), so with a bit of avian adrenalin and stretchy, plastic mesh, it's perfectly feasible for a wren to escape in the manner that it did, much as I found it hard to believe my eyes. I searched the net several times over for any broken strands of green plastic which would have aided the wren's escape, but the netting was intact.

Wren's do have stocky bodies but the bird did seem to elongate as it squeezed through the mesh. When you take into account that a square of side 1.5cm has a perimeter of 6cm, and that 6cm when transformed into a circle by the supple wren's transit through the pliable plastic, that circle has a diameter of over 1.9cm. I ought not to have been so surprised by the wren's stunt.

This was not the first time that I have been amazed at the ability of an animal to pass through a seemingly impossible gap. A few years ago, I was sitting on the toilet when a mouse came in under the locked bathroom door, ran towards me and over my bare right foot, ignoring me as if I wasn't there. The mouse disappeared down a tiny gap by a pipe. I measured the gap under the toilet door: it was 7mm, confirming the hard-to-believe anecdote that if a pencil can fit under a door, so can a mouse.

August 27th

I normally get up between eight and nine o'clock but today I was up, bright-eyed and bushy-tailed, at six o'clock. I was off to the Royal Infirmary of Edinburgh for my first knee replacement. My knees have been severely arthritic for some years as a result of decades of misuse and perhaps some added genetic tendency. My legs in my twenties were straight and true. During my forties and fifties, they became increasingly bowed so much so that a well-fed Labrador dog could have walked between them and I probably would not have noticed, unless, of course, it was wagging its tail.

I spent the morning in the orthopaedic ward undergoing tests and waiting. There were quite a few of us on the orthopaedic surgery conveyer belt and I was last in line. Maybe being the youngest with no additional health issues had something to do with that, but I got to pre-op around 1pm. If you're squeamish, miss the next paragraph.

In general and simple terms, a full knee replacement involves an eight inch incision on the front of the knee with the knee cap pushed to the side so that the damaged bones underneath are easily accessible to the surgeon. The eroded top of the tibia (shinbone) and bottom of the femur (thighbone) are cut off with great precision and removed along with the remnants of cartilage and cruciate ligaments, if you are lucky enough to still have them. You keep your lateral ligaments, medial ligaments and your kneecap. The bone surfaces which have been removed are replaced with a metal and plastic prosthesis, then the knee cap is shoved back into place and the wound stitched up.

I asked Nick, the Australian surgeon who performed my operation, if I could keep the top of my tibia. He informed me that my idea for making an amulet from the tibia-top was not going to happen for reasons of possible infection. Whether this was to protect me or other people from infection, I don't know, but I reluctantly accepted his professional judgment. Nick did say that this was the first time that he had had this request. They obviously don't make Scotch broth in Sydney.

Around 1pm, I received an injection in the base of my spine so that all sensation of pain was lost below my belly button. This was rather disconcerting because after ten minutes, I could see my toes but no matter how hard I tried to wiggle them, I couldn't raise so much as a twitch. In one way this was reassuring as the drug was doing its job, but at the same time I couldn't help feeling a bit of empathy for those who have lost the use of their lower limbs due to spinal injury.

I had been given an anaesthetic through a cannula in my arm and I was starting to get drowsy. The spinal injection removes any sensation of pain but you can still feel pressure and movement on the surface of your skin. I was told that the anaesthetic would put me to sleep. I felt manipulations around my knee and thought that this must be the medics making the incision. The sound of an electrical machine-tool and more pressure on my knee gave me the idea in my semi-conscious state that the surgical team was getting down to business with the electric saw. The anaesthetist leaned over me to check my awareness level and said, 'That's your leg shaved. We'll get you into theatre now.' Then I conked out.

On starting to regain consciousness, a nice person reassuringly informed me that all had gone well. I felt very relaxed, as you would expect given the current state of expertise in anaesthesia.

A few moments later, I was to experience a strange phenomenon which is related to a pathology called body integrity identity disorder (BIID). Sufferers of BIID believe a body part doesn't belong to them so they try to get it amputated. BIID patients would rather live as an amputee than live with a limb that they believe is not theirs. Science writer, Anil Ananthaswamy, addresses BIID, along with many other syndromes, when he discusses connections between brain, body, mind and self, and examines a range of neuropsychological complaints in his intriguing, thought-provoking and sometimes disturbing book, 'The Man Who Wasn't There: Tales from the Edge of the Self'.

So how was my mind affected? I had what I can only describe as a temporary, right-leg-integrity identity disorder, not to the extent that I wished it amputated, but the leg didn't feel as if it were mine and it certainly didn't look like mine.

24

I looked down the length of my body and, for some reason, the surgeon and his assistant were holding a leg at 45° to the operating table. This leg could not belong to me as there was absolutely no sensation of pain, pressure, touch or temperature despite the foot attached to the naked leg being hoisted a yard above the table. There was another reason that the leg could not be mine; the right leg that had supported me all my life had got bandier and bandier over the last three decades as my osteoarthritis had worsened, but this leg being held aloft was dead straight.

This temporary right-leg integrity identity disorder lasted all of about ten seconds before I put two and two together in my confused state and finally got four, by considering alternative evidence. Primarily, the leg was attached to me, and secondly, the knee had a long line of staple sutures running down it, so I concluded that the operation was over and that it was my leg. Becoming a little more rational, I enquired of Nick if there had been much left of my knee cartilage, the tough, flexible, connective tissue which acts as a cushion and aids smooth movement in joints. Nick laughed and replied that my knee was 'ivoried', which I took to mean 'no'. The surfaces of my femur and tibia had been so eroded that they had been rubbed smooth to the extent of resembling ivory. This explained some of the eerie sounds that my knee had made during the last decade when I turned too quickly, not to mention the accompanying, excruciating pain.

The way a sound is produced when two smooth surfaces rub together is very interesting. It is caused by the surfaces alternating between sticking and slipping, which generates a vibration. This phenomenon is appropriately called slip-stick, which, funnily enough, can be produced by cheap lipsticks, a slip-stick anagram. The screech of brakes is the result of slip-stick, but so is the sound of a bow on the strings of a cello, so slip-stick can be a pleasant as well as an irritating phenomenon.

You can annoy others with slip-stick by drawing your finger across a blown-up balloon or by rubbing a knife between the tines of a fork. If the discordance and frequency of these vibrations match those of primate alarm-calls (around 3500Hertz), akin to the screams of a baby in distress, we feel a primeval immediacy and heightened awareness. It is reasonable to hypothesise that this had, or still has evolutionary, survival benefits.

There could well be a reason for our sometimes irrational, angry, emotional response to the apparent pain produced by the screech of brakes or cutlery scraping a plate. Scientists, led by Sukhbinder Kumar from the Institute of Neuroscience, Newcastle University, explained this in a paper, *'Features versus Feelings: Dissociable Representations of the Acoustic Features and Valence of Aversive Sounds'*, published in the Journal of Neuroscience (October 10th, 2012). By using functional magnetic resonance imaging, Sukhbinder Kumar and colleagues have shown that such sounds caused heightened activity between parts of the brain involved in emotions, the amygdalae, and the auditory cortex which processes sound. They tested seventy four sounds on thirteen volunteers and the top five most unpleasant sounds were produced by slip-stick: a knife on a bottle; a fork on a glass; chalk on a blackboard; a ruler on a bottle; nails on a blackboard; and the sixth sound in this league table of auditory anguish was a female scream.

When we hear an unpleasant noise, the amygdalae modulate the response of the auditory cortex, increasing activity and initiating our negative reaction. Even thinking about such sounds can have a powerful effect. Pick one of the slip-stick effects mentioned above, close your eyes and imagine it happening by the side of your head. You have probably clenched your fists, gritted your teeth and hunched your shoulders; your awareness has been raised, your fight-flight response initiated and you are ready to face, or flee from, the source of the scary stimulus, and enhance your chance of survival.

August 29th

Yesterday, the day after my knee operation, was a bit of a blur. I was in a four-person ward with three other men who had undergone surgery similar to mine. We had obviously introduced ourselves but with the consumption of strong pain-killers, I couldn't remember much of what we spoke about. The same applied to the conversations that I'd had with family visitors. Which conversations had been had with whom was lost in fuzzy memory and every time I started to talk, I'd have that unpleasant feeling that I was repeating myself; déjà vu, or more accurately, déjà parlé.

'Stop me if I've already told you this,' was the most frequent statement I made, but it didn't really matter if I was speaking to the other patients as they couldn't remember whether I'd told them what I was talking about or not. They were on similar pain-killers to me.

Physiotherapists seem overly zealous at getting you up on your feet and moving around after you have had surgery, but all to speed recovery. First, a walking frame, or zimmer, is your method of support and within a day you're on to crutches or sticks. There is an interesting etymology behind the word 'zimmer'; the 'zimmer' walking frame is named after the original manufacturers, Zimmer Orthopaedic Ltd, now known as Zimmer Bionet, a company that could well have made my replacement knee as they make about a quarter of replacement knees worldwide.

Show progress in locomotion and you're off home in three or four days. The ward, just like the waiting rooms and operating theatres, was also part of the conveyer belt of getting patients in and out of hospital reasonably quickly. No sooner had a bed been vacated, stripped and thoroughly cleaned than a new patient arrived. The advice which I'd received when I came into the ward two days ago, I readily delivered to the newcomers. Take the painkillers before you get sore, or you'll regret it. There were a couple of times that I was half an hour too slow to ask for pain relief and did I regret it? But the consideration and thoughtfulness of the frontline staff who dealt with me was always sympathetic and caring.

August 30th

Today, I witnessed an act of compassion and kindness, imbued with professionalism, which supersedes anything I've seen before and probably anything which I'll likely see again.

Yesterday, a frail, elderly gentleman was brought into the ward to occupy a vacant bed. He was witty and articulate, obviously very intelligent. I could have imagined him as head master at an old-fashioned, private school, or perhaps, as a senior civil servant. On the surface, he conveyed an air of confidence, but after he had a short nap, he would wake disorientated and bewildered, not knowing his whereabouts. After a few minutes and some questions, normal service in his head was resumed.

Sometimes when he woke, he would immediately reel off our names, his fellow patients, and express delight when he got them right. This was not to show off, but to confirm to himself that he was retaining his faculties, which given his apparent intelligence, he knew were on the wane. Despite staff encouraging us all to keep curtains open, probably to avoid isolation, the gentleman liked to draw the curtain round his bed as soon as staff left the ward, as much, I felt, for security as for privacy,

After nine o'clock in the evening, the night nurse was doing her round taking temperatures and blood pressures. The night nurse had not yet met the elderly gentleman, who had been sleeping for over an hour, behind his curtain, and seemed to be in a very deep sleep. The nurse woke him and he was in a more confused and more anxious state than we had previously witnessed. He was frightened and worried.

The night nurse introduced herself and calmly explained that she knew the gentleman's name, where he came from and where he was going within the next few days. During the course of this conversation, you could hear the tension and fear in the old man's voice begin to dissipate. The nurse perceptively asked him if he normally had a room to himself to which he replied in the affirmative. She then suggested that if that was the case, it would be a good thing to keep the curtain round his bed completely closed overnight as this would help him to relax; the tension dropped another level. The night nurse took his temperature and blood pressure, all the while reassuring and settling the old man.

You could hear from the tenor of his voice that he understood exactly his confusion and how the nurse brought him mental and physical respite. When she was leaving, he thanked her profoundly and explained how she had saved him from a night of torment and anguish. In the space of five minutes, with a tender manner and careful choice of words, the night nurse had transformed a distressed elderly patient into one who was relaxed and comfortable in his unfamiliar surroundings.

I have sometimes thought about the relative meanings of pity, sympathy, empathy and compassion, and how they differ. The definitions are unimportant compared to the actions associated with these attributes and the outcomes which result from them. The night nurse certainly exhibited compassion, along with care, kindness, concern and gentle consideration. That there are people like her, who can show such quality and commitment, and act with beauty in the normal course of their daily work, should make us humble and grateful. Perhaps many of us should take a much closer look at ourselves, our actions and our motivations.

September

'By all these lovely tokens

September days are here,

With summer's best of weather

And autumn's best of cheer.'

Helen Hunt Jackson, (1830-1885)

'Few are altogether deaf to the preaching of pine trees.

Their sermons on the mountains go to our hearts;

and if people in general could be got into the woods, even for once,

to hear the trees speak for themselves,

all difficulties in the way of forest preservation would vanish.'

John Muir (1838-1914)

September 3rd

I got home from hospital three days ago. My time has been spent sleeping lots, waking up to take painkillers, hobbling around the garden on sticks and then having another snooze. This is called recuperation. The siesta-seat is an even more attractive proposition than usual, given the clement weather. The sun shines on it in the afternoon, it's wind-protected by the garden's high wall and surrounding shrubs and, best of all, it is situated under a medium-sized Scots pine, *Pinus sylvestris,* the scent of which encourages me to close my eyes; as if I needed any encouragement. *Pinus sylvestris* translates as 'pine of the woods', *sylvestris* meaning, 'of the woods'; and hence silviculture, the cultivation of trees; and Transylvania, being beyond the forest; and Pennsylvania, literally, Penn's Woods, from William Penn, for whom the state was named.

The perfume of Scots pine evokes freshness and woodland walks, the scent a complex mix of volatile chemicals which has evolved to protect the pine from the ravages of bacteria, fungi and herbivores, large and small. The major components of the coniferous essence are chemical compounds called terpenes, such as alpha- and beta-pinene, and aromatic esters such as bornyl acetate: these are the chief volatiles which dominate the fresh fragrance, so fresh that these compounds are added to air-fresheners and cleaners to imbue our homes with an atmosphere of nature and health. Terpenes are a large group of organic chemicals which form a main component of pine tree resin and turpentine, a liquid used as a solvent and obtained by distillation of tree resin, usually that of pine trees.

The needles, twigs and cones from the Scots pine are used to make an essential oil, pine oil, through a process called steam distillation, a special type of distillation, more delicate than ordinary distillation. This is used for temperature-sensitive materials like natural, aromatic products. Pine oil has been traditionally used in inhalants or as cough medicine ingredients to treat chronic, bronchial problems and catarrh, as it exhibits antiseptic, secretolytic and expectorant properties. The oil is sometimes applied to the skin to relieve muscle ache, and like all embrocations, if it smells as if it should do you good, its placebo effect certainly will be doing you good.

Alternative medicine practitioners suggest that pine is beneficial in treating despondency and despair. As most days, I spend time sitting or lying beneath my pine tree, I must be availing myself of its efficacious properties. Whether this accounts for my lack of despondency and despair, I would hazard to guess, because as far as I'm concerned, alternative medicine is an alternative to other types of medicine, types which, through double-blind, clinical trials, have been proven to work.

I don't decry pine oil's therapeutic qualities as there are some clinical studies which have concluded that pine has antipruritic, anti-inflammatory, antibacterial and antifungal properties; but I would assert that these studies do not have the validity of a randomised, double-blind, placebo-controlled, clinical trial. Anyway, I'm relaxed when I snooze under my *Pinus sylvestris,* so whether the results are due to the placebo effect, a benefit based on belief, or to benefits accruing from active constituents in the air under my pine tree is a moot point.

A while ago, I trimmed some of the lower branches from the pine tree. A week later, small drops of resin had formed where I had removed a branch. In the spirit of clinical research, I licked the resin. There was no initial taste, but after a few seconds, I was hit with astringency like strong, bitter, black tea, probably due to tannins in the resin. This was followed by an aftertaste of cough sweets which lasted for a good hour, not a particularly unpleasant taste. It's unwise to taste stuff from your garden unless you are reasonably confident that it is non-toxic.

On the other hand, it can be quite exciting:

'All the world is a laboratory to the inquiring mind.'

Martin Henry Fischer (1879-1962)

September 4th

Once again, after lunch, beneath the pine tree, I was enjoying a satisfying and restorative, sun- and drug-induced sleep, unaware of the aggravation to come.

There is an insect called a flower bug because its scientific name, *Anthocoris nemorum,* means exactly that: from the Greek, 'anthus', for 'flower' and 'koris' for 'bug', and *nemorum* meaning 'of the pasture'. It is small, up to about 5mm long, and feeds on other small creatures such as aphids, but is perfectly happy to bite a human. *Anthocoris nemorum* is not all bad as it is used as a biological control of thrips, small insects which damage commercial crops. The only thing of interest about thrips is that the word 'thrips', like sheep or grouse, is both the singular and the plural of the beasts. You can have one thrips or two thrips, and one sheep or two sheep, but here's a tangential thought: if you have one mouse or louse, and two mice or lice, shouldn't the plural of grouse be grice?

In Scotland, *Anthocoris nemorum* are often referred to as berry bugs because they are most active during the berry-picking season from July to September. As this is when people and berry bugs are most likely to come into contact, it is at this time that people are most likely to notice the bugs' carnivorous proclivity. The bugs are active from mid-February, when hibernating adults are roused by early spring warmth in the suntraps where I like to sit, and they continue to be active right through to October, in my unfortunate itchy and scratchy experience.

Berry bug bites are fairly easy to recognise because you will have a row of them which follows a line of tight clothing, such as knickerelastic or the top of tight socks, and often under watch straps. The bug creeps into the constricted area and uses the pressure above to help push its piercing and sucking, three-segmented beak into your skin. This apparatus is normally used to inject prey with digestive enzymes and to suck up the resultant liquids. On humans, after the initial bite, the bug then moves along an inch or so before repeating the penetrating performance. Little is felt until later, sometimes the following day, when you touch the small bite-mark and immediately initiate a histamine reaction, causing itch and irritation as bad as a bite from a mosquito.

There are some of us who have a genetic disposition to react more severely than others to certain types of insect bite. I, sadly, react badly to the bites of mosquitoes and berry bugs, much to the amusement of members of my family whose reactions are much milder. As a child, I remember getting such bites and my mother, convinced that I'd caught a flea, would place me in the empty bath, put in the plug then strip me naked. She would then shake out all my clothes in an attempt to find the offending flea but, of course, she never did.

Thirty years ago, after the birth of my elder daughter, Kirsten, I discovered that Sudocream, a proprietary product to treat nappy rash, was very effective at diminishing the itch of both berry bug and mosquito bites. Other brands of nappy rash treatments may be as equally effective.

Around ten years ago, I was serendipitously bitten on the upper arm right next to a pain receptor in my skin, so my attention was immediately drawn to the culprit. It was the time of year when berry bugs were prevalent so I exercised self-control and didn't immediately squish the guilty party. I let the blighter bite, and the scientist in me hoped that if the bite developed into that which I recognised as a berry bug bite, then I would finally be able to associate this bug with these bites which have caused me irritation for so long.

The bite developed like all the rest had previously and I identified the bug as the flower bug, *Anthocoris nemorum.* I further ascertained that *Anthocoris nemorum* is closely related to the bed bug, *Cimex lectularius,* so it should come as no great surprise that the flower bug has an admirable ability to pierce human skin and cause severe irritation.

Now we reach 'the aggravation to come' which I mentioned earlier. After my surgery, it was a prerequisite to wear anti-embolism stockings on both legs. These stockings are tight, knee-length socks that lower the risk of post-operative, deep vein thrombosis. This can cause pain and swelling in the leg and lead to complications such as a pulmonary embolism, a condition which occurs when a blood clot breaks off into the bloodstream and then blocks one of the blood vessels in the lungs.

This afternoon, while I slept peacefully under the pine tree, a bloody berry bug, as I on occasion alliteratively refer to them, got up my trouser leg and under my anti-embolism stocking. It delivered seven bites of which I knew nothing, until four o'clock in the morning when I unconsciously started rubbing them. They reacted, like they always do with me, by itching horrendously. The purposefully tight, anti-embolism stockings (only removed for showering) exacerbated the itch to such a level that a Spanish inquisitor would have been in rapture if he could have inflicted such torment upon a victim.

During this last week, I had, at various times, experienced muscle pain, bone pain, referred pain and general discomfort until I was usually rescued by appropriate analgesic medication. None of these pains caused me anything like the suffering brought about by the combination of *Anthocoris nemorum* and anti-embolism socks. If you are lucky enough to have the genetics so that you are unaffected by *Anthocoris nemorum*, the berry bug, be very, very grateful to those who bequeathed you those genes, otherwise always have available the panacea that is Sudocream. (Other brands of nappy rash treatments may be as equally effective.)

September 8th

It's time to get my staples out. These are the metallic sutures which have held together the eight-inch, vertical wound over my knee. They are similar to large office staples but when inserted, they are bent in the middle so that the sides go into your skin at an angle towards each other so that the staple would have difficulty falling out: imagine a wire pentagon with one of its sides missing.

A nurse in the orthopaedics department at the hospital kindly gave me a sealed, sterile device which looked like a cross between a pair of tweezers and a set of small pliers with a hooked end. I was to take it with me when I attended my local medical practice to have the staples removed by the practice nurse at the doctors' surgery. The hospital staff may have been unaware that a surgery's practice nurse can often be busier than the doctors in a practice and that getting an appointment can be rather difficult. Government and National Health Service policy has tried to free up general practitioners' time by having practice nurses perform duties that were once only the doctors' privilege. This works if the practice is adequately resourced to provide enough nurse-hours to cope with demand.

Yesterday, I had tried to get an appointment with the practice nurse but she was fully booked. I had asked to book an appointment for today but was told that this wasn't policy and I would have to phone back on the morning of the day on which I wanted the appointment. I duly did early this morning only to be told that once again there was no appointment available, despite me explaining that some of the staples were getting rather gooey round the edges. I politely enquired if a doctor could be available to perform the staple-removal.

There was some humming and hawing until I said that there was no need to worry if a doctor's appointment was not available. I could quite easily take out the staples myself as I had the staple-removers and was perfectly happy to give it a go. An appointment, strangely enough, was immediately found to be available.

A pleasant, young, male doctor, new to the practice, efficiently removed my thirty staples, leaving sixty pinprick holes, each quarter of an inch deep. My knee looked like it had been fastened shut with a thick, eight-inch zip.

September 10th

Early Brussels sprouts are a delicious, mild-flavoured vegetable and I enjoyed the first pick today. There is a satisfying pleasure in picking your own sprouts straight from the garden and putting them into the steamer with no more than a quick wash. A greater proportion of soluble nutrients are retained when vegetables are steamed as opposed to boiled. Why? Because, when vegetables are cooked in boiling water, they are moved, bruised and bashed around. This damages the walls of the plant cells releasing vitamins and minerals into the water. For this reason, my granny-in-law used drink the residual water left after vegetables had been boiled, a trait I have inherited through marriage.

September 14th

It has been two weeks since I got home from hospital. I'd expected to be able to get lots of reading done but all that I've managed to do is open books, read for ten minutes, then lose concentration and fall asleep. Whether this is my body demanding rest to recuperate or the somnific effect of the pain-killers, I don't know, probably a combination of both. The information given during the pre-med interview, a couple of weeks before the surgery, did inform that recovery would demand more sleep than usual. Somehow, I seemed to think that I'd have some sort of say about how much extra sleep I'd need and when it should occur, but nature, or medication, has decided otherwise.

I've been in what my mother used to call a dwam, a dozy, dreamy, relaxed state where you just let time look after itself. The word, 'dwam', derives from the Old English, 'dwolma', meaning 'confusion', or from the Middle Dutch, 'dwelm', meaning 'stupefaction', but probably both if one was derived from the other or both derived from the same root. I feel another dwam coming on and you, reading this paragraph, probably do as well.

After two weeks, you'd be forgiven if you thought boredom might have kicked in. Maybe it has, but I'm lucky. I'm not particularly prone to boredom and I don't know if I'd be able to recognise it. This was explained to me when I read in New Scientist magazine an article called, *'Bored? Well don't be'* (August 29th, 2015). A scientist called Thomas Goetz, from the University of Konstanz, reckons that there are five types of boredom: indifferent, apathetic, calibrating, searching and reactant.

If I experience boredom then it is the first type, indifferent, the least negative type of boredom, a benign type, where you tend to remain relaxed, in a contented...... dwam, I suppose? This is the best kind of boredom, the kind that can result in unexpected, creative thinking.

Apathetic boredom leaves you feeling as if you are unable to do anything about your situation, resulting in depression and helplessness; an unpleasant type of boredom.

Calibrating boredom is much like apathetic boredom, but you keep hoping something will turn up, but you don't make much effort; you live in hope.

Searching boredom is a form in which you feel restless and actively look for ways to lessen your boredom, but if you fail you can fall into the worst kind of boredom, reactant boredom.

In reactant boredom, there is a combination of energy and negativity, but with no outlet, it leaves you feeling angry and aggressive; like the bored, frustrated adolescent who blames anyone and everything for their malcontent.

I am lucky in, and indifferent to, my boredom. Indifference lets the mind wander and ponder on nothing in particular; or many things in particular, sometimes sequentially and at other times holistically. A relaxed wandering and pondering mind, like a tranquil traveller, can have an enlightened perception of their environment and appreciate ideas that may once have seemed alien. If unfamiliar ideas are given enough time to be assimilated and viewed from different perspectives, not only might you learn more from these untried angles, you might learn more about yourself.

September 18th

Today's my birthday. I don't see birthdays as any different from any other day; if you wake up and something hurts, you're still alive. I have no need of birthday presents as I have everything that I need and want, but my wife and daughters insist on buying me stuff. Some of it sits secretly in a drawer for years, and after around a decade, it somehow finds its way to a charity shop. I do appreciate their thoughtfulness, but there surely must be more worthy ways to spend their money than to spend it on a thankless old git like me.

This year, I've made an arrangement with them and they pooled the birthday money. This was used to buy stuff for two local food banks. I can't think of a more worthwhile birthday present. Some good has been done and I have made no personal effort. Is this confirmation of my goodness or my laziness? Am I an old curmudgeon for considering birthdays and Christmas an excuse for profligate indulgence?

If you believe the old aphorism that it is better to give than to receive, then donating your birthday present to a food bank does both simultaneously. Now, could that be some sort of egocentric self-indulgence?

September 19th

Yesterday, I cut the front grass and then went for a walk; well more of a stroll, for about an hour, and today my legs are telling me that I overdid it. The grass wasn't a problem as my mower is petrol-driven, so grass-cutting is like walking the lawn with a zimmer. Maybe I was on my feet for longer than I should have been and muscles which have been underused for the past month were certainly complaining. As my bandy leg has been straightened by around ten degrees at the knee, some muscles on the inside of my right quadriceps have been stretched and they were particularly achy.

Rest was required, and given that the Rugby World Cup is currently being played, I watched four games today. The last ten minutes of Japan against South Africa almost had me jumping out of my seat; it would have if I had been capable. Japan won with the last play of the game, delighting rugby fans around the world, unless they were South African.

September 23rd

I was checked over by a physiotherapist yesterday and I was pleased to be informed that I was making very good progress. The exercises which I had been advised to do by the hospital physiotherapist had obviously helped my recuperation and I was shown some extra exercises that would further aid my recovery.

Today is much more auspicious than a simple visit to the physiotherapist. It is the autumnal equinox, one of the four most astronomically important events in the calendar year and it has been recognised as such for at least 5000 years, probably more. There are over twenty megalithic cairns or passage tombs, dating to around 3000 BCE, at Loughcrew, County Meath in Ireland. Passages in two of these cairns are aligned to receive light from the rising sun on both the autumnal and vernal (spring) equinoxes. Sunbeams shine down the main passage and illuminate ancient artwork of solar symbols on the backstone at the end of the passage opposite the entrance. The intelligent and resourceful folks who built these monuments were stone-age people and they had an understanding of materials, construction, light, time and astronomy, probably much more so than most people today.

Day and night are of roughly equal length at an equinox, derived from the Latin for 'equal night'. The earth orbits the sun once a year, spinning on its axis tilted at 23° to its orbit. Only twice during this orbit does the plane of the earth's equator pass through the centre of the sun so that the sun is positioned exactly overhead on the equator. This results in an equinox, one in the spring around March 20th and one in the autumn around September 23rd. The autumnal equinox marks the beginning of the astronomical definition of autumn, as opposed to September 1st which is the start of the meteorological autumn.

So why two starts to autumn, and winter, spring and summer for that matter? Astronomical seasons are based on the Earth's position in relation to the sun. The meteorological seasons are based on the annual temperature cycle, starting about three weeks earlier than their astronomical equivalents. Astronomical seasons vary in length, so the start date of a new season can fall on a different date each year, making it difficult to compare the seasons' climate records over different years; so the meteorological calendar was introduced. This cuts the calendar into four seasons of almost equal duration.

I shall celebrate the autumnal equinox by performing the new exercises, suggested yesterday by the physiotherapist, with the hope that full recovery will be achieved by the vernal equinox in approximately six months' time. As I was to discover in early March, this was to be some hope.

September 25th

John Keats described autumn as the season of mists and mellow fruitfulness, and today was archetypal of that delicate description. The late-September, early-morning sun was low-angled, somewhat south of east, trying vainly to evaporate the dew from the myriad of small, spangled spiders' webs adorning the grass. What warmth the sun gave was countered by the dampness in the still air. Due to this moisture, my breath hung as clouds and the moist air seemed to enhance the scents of the wet earth and grass. Half-rotten and squirrel-gnawed fruit under the James Grieve apple tree tainted the atmosphere with a piquant perfume of cider vinegar and fresh decay.

As I wandered the corners inspecting the garden's more secret places, I could hear the melancholic sound of migrating geese approaching from the north. I walked to the middle of the grass to get a better view and saw about eighty geese heading roughly south-west. For me, geese flying southwards in their characteristic V-formation is the unarguable harbinger of seasonal change. For how many millennia have men like me looked upwards at a skein of geese flying south and heard their plaintive honk, only to feel winter's cold fingers caress the back of their neck.

I blanked the traffic sound and blinkered my eyes from brick and stone buildings. I could see only the sky and the goose chevron, and I imagined what people in the past might have felt. Would the Mesolithic hunter-gatherer, the Neolithic cairn-builder in Loughcrew, the Roman, the Saxon, or the Scot on his runrig have felt any differently from how I did today? At the sound and sight of the geese, would they have shivered involuntarily, not at the day's damp chill, but at the winter to come? If autumnal melancholy has a sound, it is the despondent honk of geese, high overhead, flying south to their winter grazing, leaving their frozen north behind.

A skein of migratory geese exhibits how evolution has maximised the efficiency of their energy usage in flight, in ways similar to that adopted by cycling teams during the Tour de France. When a cyclist moves, turbulence is produced in the form of vortices, eddies of air behind them. This causes low pressure areas creating drag, a force which slows cyclists and against which they must peddle harder to maintain speed.

If a second cyclist moves into the space directly behind the first cyclist, the low pressure area will pull the second cyclist along because as the air in the vortices rotate from the outside in, the air-movement pushes the second cyclist along. Cyclists call this drafting and, counter-intuitively, it benefits the first cyclist as well as the second. By occupying the space behind the first cyclist, the second cyclist cuts the first's drag. The first cyclist still needs to work harder than the second, but not as hard as if they were cycling on their own.

Cyclists in a race form a pack called a peloton where everyone except the lead cyclist benefits from riding in someone else's slipstream. A cyclist within the peloton can use up to around 50% less energy than a cyclist alone.

Things get more interesting if there is a crosswind. Rather than ride in a peloton, cyclists will ride in an echelon, a diagonal line of cyclists, where the lead rider fights the wind, let's say coming from the front and to the right. The second rider will cycle behind and to the left, in the lee of the lead cyclist. When it is time to change the lead cyclist, the front rider peels off to the right and moves back round the echelon to attach on the rear.

And so it is with geese. Flocks are equipped by evolution to fly in an energetically efficient V-formation, but in a manner which is more complex than that of the cyclists. The cyclists' peloton is confined to moving within two dimensions, discounting the up and down of the road; geese have the freedom to fly in all three spatial dimensions. Not only do geese fly in the wake of other birds, behind and to the side, but they also continually adjust their vertical position to gain advantage from the updraft from the upbeat of the bird's wings in front; and they actively avoid the downdraft from the downbeat.

What's more, each goose times its own wing beat to be slightly out of time to that of the bird in front. This maximises their efficiency so that a flock flying like this can increase its range by up to 70%. When a flock of geese are at a distance and you view it as it flies towards or away from you, you may be lucky enough to see a Mexican wave move along the line of geese, created by their slightly-out-of-time wing beats.

If you see a V-skein of geese which is asymmetric or even completely lacking one side, there is probably a strong crosswind. Rather than a skein, you have an echelon of geese, behaving just as an echelon of cyclists would, and for the same reasons.

September 28th

There are few times when the ageing process results in an awe-inspiring experience.

As the years have slipped by, one of the less agreeable aspects of increasing maturity is the greater frequency of toilet trips in the small hours of the night. Not that I object to these obligatory visits as the alternative could be messy and should be avoided. However, in the early hours of this morning, I was fortunate to receive Nature's call in time to witness a wonderful, astronomical combination of events.

A total lunar eclipse was occurring while the moon was at its perigee, the closest point to the Earth in its orbit. The moon's orbit is not circular, but elliptical, and the Earth is off-centre, being closer to one end of the ellipse than the other. When the moon is at its perigee, a full moon is described as a supermoon due to the perceived increase in size, and when the moon is at its furthest from Earth, at its apogee, the apogean full moon is called a micromoon.

A supermoon is 14% larger and 30% brighter than a micromoon, but the brightness is obviously irrelevant during an eclipse, as was occurring tonight. The combination of a supermoon with a total lunar eclipse was last seen in Edinburgh in 1982 and won't be seen again until 2033, so it was worthwhile going out the back of the house at 4am to view the spectacle, after my toilet visit. I couldn't possibly combine the two in case neighbours also had the desire to see this astronomical marvel.

A normal full moon occurs when the moon is opposite the sun with the Earth between, in the same plane but not directly in a straight line between the sun and moon. The side of the moon facing the Earth is fully illuminated by the sun and sunlight is reflected back towards the Earth. This gives us the shining, silvery, circular moon so loved by romantics, vampires and were-wolves.

A lunar eclipse occurs when the Earth is more or less exactly between the sun and moon, with the Earth blocking the sun's light from falling on the moon's surface as the moon moves through the Earth's shadow.

Such a dry description of a full moon and an eclipse does not do justice to the amazing sight of the full supermoon, as big a moon as anyone on Earth can witness. Further, this is transformed to a blood moon by the Earth's shadow, which, as it encroaches on the moon's surface, alters the moon's colour from a shining, white radiance to an eerie, reddish- brown colour. In the past, a blood moon was an ill omen, a portent of doom and destruction to the superstitious, so, any unexplained disaster which happens anywhere in the world, at any time in the next month must, of course, be due to the influence of this wondrous, celestial event.

The blood moon can be looked at in a different light. I saw it, as most scientifically minded would, as the consequence of two optical phenomena, as viewed from here on planet Earth. As sunlight passes through our planet's atmosphere, particles in the atmosphere scatter this light, but unequally. Light from the blue end of the spectrum is dispersed more readily than light from the red end of the spectrum (this is the reason why the sky is blue, but that's a story for another time), so red light passes through the Earth's atmosphere, bypassing the Earth, and travels on into space. If this light-scattering phenomenon was the only one at play, the moon would be almost black during an eclipse, but this is not the case. The Earth's atmosphere also acts like a lens, bending the red light round the Earth and into the Earth's shadow, causing the moon to blush red as if it's been caught naked in the dark.

The moon would have blushed an even brighter red if the Calbuco volcano in Chile hadn't erupted back in April, chucking dust, ash and sulphuric acid into the atmosphere. This has hung around in the stratosphere for the past five months absorbing sunlight, and continued to do so last night. Scientists reckon that the moon's redness would have been a third stronger during the eclipse if it hadn't been for Calbuco's eruption and its light-absorbing pollution.

Now with the wings of imagination, take flight, to the surface of the moon about 226,000 miles away. You are standing in bright sunlight on the surface of the moon looking towards Earth, a dark circle in its own umbra. When the eclipse begins, as the Earth's shadow encroaches on the moon, what would you see?

The Earth would appear black against the brightness of the sun just before the sun's disc started to disappear behind the Earth. Earth seems much larger than the sun because the sun is so very far away compared to the Earth. Around you, it would start to grow darker, but as your eyes became accustomed to the diminishing light, you would see your surroundings under a ghostly, red glow.

As you look to Earth, hoping for salvation from this magic, you would perceive our planet ringed by a circle of red, a crimson corona, that red light which was refracted by our atmosphere. You might even feel rather special when you realise that this red ring surrounding the Earth is the sum total of all the glow and glory of every sunset and sunrise occurring on Earth at that single moment in time: and you are the only person ever to witness this. How long would it last?

A central lunar eclipse is a relatively rare eclipse during which the moon passes through the centre of the Earth's shadow. The moon is in the Earth's umbra, its full shadow, for a hundred minutes, when the light from all twilights and dawns, seen and unseen on Earth, are directed at you.

The mind's eye can take you to impossible places. The ticket to travel is nothing more than a little knowledge and a fertile imagination. A hundred minutes on the moon might pass quite quickly with such a stupendous spectacle to entertain you, but ten minutes moon-watching on a chilly, clear night was more than enough for me and my bladder.

'The moon is friend for the lonesome to talk to.'

Carl Sandburg (1878-1967)

October

'The sweet calm sunshine of October, now

Warms the low spot; upon its grassy mold

The purple oak-leaf falls; the birchen bough

drops its bright spoil like arrow-heads of gold.'

William Cullen Bryant (1794-1878)

'In the garden, Autumn is, indeed the crowning glory of the year, bringing us the fruition of

months of thought and care and toil. And at no season, safe perhaps in Daffodil time, do we

get such superb colour effects as from August to November.'

Rose G. Kingsley (1845-1925)

'There is no season when such pleasant and sunny spots may be lighted on, and produce so

pleasant an effect on the feelings, as now in October.'

Nathaniel Hawthorne (1804-1864)

October 1ˢᵗ

It's now five weeks since my knee operation. Today, I was up and down the house stairs at least ten times, now without a stick, but with a firm grip of the banister. As I was feeling a bit smug at my progress, I got out my bike and cycled a few hundred yards to gauge the flexibility of my knee. It felt a bit tight so I raised the bicycle seat a little so I didn't need to bend my knee so much. I cycled the mile round to friends, Jim and Morag. Jim happened to be looking out his living room window. The expression on Jim's face when he spotted me on my bike was one of surprise. I tried not to look too out of breath, but over a month of purposely sitting about to allow sensible healing and recovery, despite a few half-mile walks, had certainly compromised my cardiovascular system.

Morag likes archaeology and my excuse for getting out on the bike was to lend her a book, *'Divining Archaeology'*, by Walter Elliot, a self-described mild eccentric, but an amateur archaeologist of some note and an admirable historian. He hails from my home town of Selkirk in the Scottish Borders and he is also one of my heroes. Mild eccentric he may be, but he is also the recipient of one of the most prestigious awards for Scottish archaeologists, the Dorothy Marshall Medal, presented every three years by the Council of the Society of Antiquaries of Scotland for an outstanding contribution, in a voluntary capacity, to Scottish archaeology, or related work.

Walter Elliot has an intimate knowledge of the Borders. He **knows** the land and can interpret its bumps and lumps like few others. Thirty-three years as a fencing contractor all over the Scottish Borders allowed him to observe the imprints and echoes of early settlements preserved in ditches and embankments. Walter's knowledge, understanding and interpretations of the land are beautifully presented in his book, *'Selkirkshire and The Borders, A personal view of the archaeology and history as seen by Walter Elliot, Book One, From the Beginning of Time to AD 1603'*.

It is a personal view worth visiting. The year 1603 is highly significant and seems an excellent stopping point for Walter's first volume of Selkirkshire history. 1603 saw the Union of the Crowns, where James VI of Scotland succeeded to the thrones of England and Ireland with the death of Elizabeth I of England, the last Tudor monarch. Walter's Book Two extends from 1603 to 1815, the year the Napoleonic Wars ended.

Both Morag and Jim can appreciate a good history book, but after coffee, as I charily mounted my bicycle to leave, Morag gave me a rather sceptical look. I don't know if she was questioning the subject of the book, *'Divining Archaeology'*, or my mode of transport, given my recent surgery.

October 3rd

The unseasonably good weather appears to be drawing to a close and the first substantial rain for almost three weeks is forecast. This has motivated me to scarify the front grass which I do most years around this time, preferring to do it by hand rather than machine. Why spend time and money going to a gym to keep fit when you can get equal or even better physical benefits through manual work in your own garden; if you're lucky enough to have a garden.

The Royal Horticultural Society advocates serious scarifying in the autumn as opposed to the spring as scarifying at the start of the growing season can tear up young grass shoots before their roots have had time to strengthen, and they won't recover during summer growing conditions. Scarifying has nothing to do with scaring the grass though most manual scarifying rakes are pretty scary-looking implements. Scarifying involves vigorously raking out of thatch, the old dead grass and moss which form a layer which impedes water and nutrient penetration, detrimental to both the health and appearance of the grass.

The lawn, loosely so-called, at the front of the house always seems to lose verdure during the summer months and ends up looking particularly patchy around September. I can never decide whether the yellowing patches and poor growth are caused by lack of water and too much sun, or by pests. Too much sun may appear a strange suggestion, given Scotland's weather, but the house's south-west facing front wall absorbs and then radiates heat on to the grass, adding to the heat which the grass already receives directly from the sun.

Maybe the cause is pest related. The larvae of the daddy longlegs, or crane fly, are called leatherjackets. These horrors can be over an inch long and eat the grass's roots making it more susceptible to drought.

The probability is that there is more than one cause of my chlorotic grass and the question needs asked if any cure justifies the cost, be it economic or environmental. Should I water more during the summer? Should I use a genus-specific pesticide, one that attacks only the genus *Tipula,* the crane flies? Maybe I should just let nature take its course as the grass seems to look moderately acceptable for most of the year. Should lots of clean water and questionable chemicals be employed to maintain what is effectively the least natural aspect of my garden, the monoculture that is a lawn?

October 4th

My body aches. Delayed Onset Muscle Soreness, or DOMS, is the ache you get in untrained, overworked muscles, sometimes several days after the muscle abuse. It takes me back over thirty years to pre-season, rugby-training when quadriceps, hamstrings, biceps and triceps, under-used through the summer off-season, were toned up through vigorous exercise which often involved a bit of delayed pain. DOMS is ache triggered by unaccustomed exercise causing micro-tears in muscle fibres. This results in inflammation and swelling in the muscle with the accompanying cascade of histamines and prostaglandins, your body's biochemical response to damaged tissue.

Your muscles experience dull pain with tenderness and stiffness which should, depending on how much you have over-exercised, dissipate within a few days, but if you have seriously overdone the exercise, you may suffer for a week. Once the DOMS has gone, if such exercise is repeated, muscles adapt and get stronger, preventing further damage and the associated soreness. This is the training effect.

My cycle ride of three days ago, plus yesterday's scarifying, have challenged back, arm and leg muscles which have been underused for six weeks, perhaps a lot longer. These aches are healthy aches. Unhealthy aches are those which come on suddenly, often after what may seem a minor twinge, and could indicate more severe muscle or ligament damage. Such soft-tissue injuries will worsen with repeated use and must be rested and allowed to recuperate. Trying to put up with pain after a sudden-onset injury, risks further damage to the tissue. Decades of experience of exercise, injury and ache has allowed me to discriminate between healthy and unhealthy pain, but I frequently still screw up.

As you age, it's safer to treat all soft-tissue injuries, even those which you think are trivial, as non-trivial, thus preventing them from becoming more serious. If you have a serious soft-tissue injury, you'll probably know about it, being unable to continue with what you are doing and perhaps screaming for assistance. In such situations, Accident and Emergency is your best bet.

So how can you look after your own trivial, or not so trivial, soft-tissue injuries? The worst thing you can do is to apply heat, either through a heat-rub or a hot bath, to supposedly relieve the discomfort. This may give initial relief but will exacerbate the symptoms and lengthen recuperation time. Heat brings blood to the damaged tissue which then bleeds into the surrounding areas increasing swelling, stiffness and bruising.

As a rugby player in my latter years, Tom Schofield, the club doctor and an expert in sports medicine, was crucial in improving my understanding of injury, its avoidance and its management. Tom advocated RICE for the treatment of soft-tissue injuries: not the pudding, but the acronym for Rest, Ice, Compression and Elevation, all intended to reduce the amount of bleeding within damaged tissue and so reduce the time required to regain full fitness. Heat does the very opposite in the first thirty six hours after injury. Thirty years on, I still use Tom's protocol, and it works. Thanks, Tom.

October 8th

As daylight hours start to noticeably diminish and the temperatures, some days, hardly reach double figures (°C), my favourite genus of shrubs becomes my objects of early autumnal contemplation. The viburnums elicit warmth and delight as others lose their sparkle. This genus has no complicated derivation to its name as in ancient times, 'viburnum' was the Latin name for the Wayfaring-tree, *Viburnum lantana*. It got the Wayfaring appellation as it was to be seen alongside roads and pathways, common in hedges.

I'm not the only person to appreciate viburnums, as history shows. The Iceman, Otzi, was discovered in melting, glacial ice in 1991 in the eponymous Otztal Alps near the border between Austria and Italy. He died 5200 years ago and his gear included a quiver full of arrows, the shafts of some made from the Wayfarer-tree or its cousin, the Guelder rose, *Viburnum opulus*. Both these shrubs throw up straight growth, suitable for arrows, from basal shoots which grow from buds at the bottom of the bush, or from dormant buds on the roots.

I don't have a *Viburnum lantana* in my garden but I do have a *Viburnum opulus*. The garden Guelder rose is a *Viburnum* cultivar that is believed to have originated in the Dutch province of Gelderland. A rose, however, it certainly is not. Its flowers come in clusters called inflorescences, with small fertile flowers in the centre, surrounded by a ring of showy, sterile flowers. These outer flowers have two possible evolutionary purposes in that, one, they act as an attractant to insect pollinators, luring them in to pollinate the fertile flowers; and two, they can also be the sacrificed to any browsing herbivore that fancies the flower's colour or smell. This results in minimal loss to the plants reproductive capacity, as the central seed-producers are less likely to be damaged.

The fertilised flowers produce a drupe, a fruit that contains a single seed which, if eaten, will be dispersed by the consumer after passing through its digestive system. It is wise to leave this fruit to the birds because the drupe of the Guelder rose is bitter and may cause sickness and diarrhoea, being mildly toxic. It has, however, been used in the past for relief of period pains, hence an alternative common name for the plant, cramp bark, which indicates that it is perhaps the bark that is the panacea and not the fruit.

It's neither the fruit nor the flowers of *Viburnum opulus* which I like, but the leaves. They have the shape of small maple leaves but with three lobes as opposed to the maple's five. Their autumn colour comes early. At a distance, the green foliage initially appears to turn an orange-peach colour, but on closer inspection, the prominent veins remain green while the parts in between the veins are a deep maroon. This combination of the green and maroon give the illusion of peachiness, and as the days pass, the maroon spreads to the leaf veins and the colour at distance changes from its early orange-peach towards claret, through burgundy to chestnut brown.

'Maroon' is derived from French for chestnut, 'marron', and, in turn, from the Medieval Greek, 'maraon'. When the October sun kisses these autumnal colours and the dappled chiaroscuro of the leaf shadow dances on the grass, it's easy to be transported from the banalities of the day and lose yourself in the beauty of the garden's light and colour spectacular.

If your garden can take a fifteen-foot shrub, then *Viburnum opulus* will bring you delight, but beware its spreading nature. The easiest and cheapest way to get your own Guelder rose is to break off a few small branches from any you find in a neighbour's garden, with the owner's permission of course. Pot them up, keep them moist in a shady spot and you will be rewarded with at least one of them, and likely more, demonstrating the ability of *Viburnum opulus* to develop roots and produce an independent plant, a clone of the one from which your branches were procured.

There are two other *Viburnums* that tickle my senses at this time of year. One of these is the *Viburnum farreri*, named after the plant collector, Reginald Farrer, and has been sometimes called *Viburnum fragrens*, which gives a clue to one of its sensory attractions. It grows to ten feet tall with a six foot spread, bearing clusters of white, pink-tinged flowers from late September, through winter, until April, even May. The glorious perfume which the blossom exudes tends to be more obvious in the evening, especially when the temperature is not too low. My *Viburnum farreri* is by my front gate and when I return from an evening at a local hostelry, I like to press my face gently against its flower clusters and inhale the sweet, heady bouquet, as intoxicating than anything consumed earlier. This, however, can be embarrassing.

I have had to explain to passers-by what I was doing inside a gate, in a bush, in the dark, late at night. They usually nod, give a sceptical smile and move on rather quickly. I doubt they believed me. I can hear them thinking that old Scots response where two positives make a negative, 'Aye, right.'

The other *Viburnum* is an interesting, but common, creation called *Viburnum x bodnantense* (pronounced bod-nan-tens-ee). It is a hybrid which was produced by crossing *Viburnum farreri* and *Viburnum grandiflorum,* the Himalayan viburnum.

The *Viburnum x bodnantense* was produced at Bodnant Garden, Tal-y-Cafn, North Wales in the nineteen-thirties, hence the hybrid's name. The cultivar, or variety, which I have, is called 'Dawn', kindly donated to me by my pal Maria. She is a most efficient collector of cuttings from friends' gardens, with assumed permission, she just can't help herself; she is the original cliptomaniac.

The two foot sapling, gifted by Maria, took three years to grow to five feet and produce its first flowers, pinker than *Viburnum farreri,* and larger, due to the genes of *Viburnum grandiflorum,* as '*grandiflorum*' suggests. It has a similar exhilarating fragrance to that of *Viburnum farreri.* The oval, well-veined leaves of both *Viburnum farreri* and *Viburnum* x *bodnantense* are coppery-coloured when they sprout in the spring, going green in the summer sun, before turning yellow, orange and red, to fall by the end of October, leaving their flowers to enthral you for the next six months.

October 12th

Sometimes the siesta-seat is not a peaceful place. Sound intrudes. I try to disregard the inevitable city sounds of traffic noise, and the clunks, clatters and whines associated with construction sites in the vicinity. Today, the siesta-seat *is* a peaceful place as a light wind is caressing the upper branches of the birch trees in my garden and those of the poplar tree next door. As the leaves are no longer connected to the trees' nutrient transport systems, but only to twigs by the last threads lignin and cellulose, the leaves have lost their water supply and have dried out. They await their disconnection, descent to the ground and their slow decay.

Those stubborn leaves which cling to their twigs provide a whispering, percussive sound which masks the grating disturbance of humans' work and communication. The rustle of the drying leaves is different from that produced when the leaves sport their summer green. Summer-leaf sounds are delicate like the hiss of sugar poured from a sachet, but today, the sounds are less subtle as the dried leaves brush against each other and against the twigs that still carry them. It's like a light rain on a windowsill. Each of the individual, leaf collisions seem separate, differentiated, unlike in the summer, when the soft contacts coalesce to a hypnotic, white noise.

I lay there in my usual, lunchtime's postprandial place, eyes closed. I was trying to decide whether the sound of the leaves caressing each other was that of gentle rain on windows, or of drizzle on the top of a tent, enjoying that warm sense of protection from the elements you get when the pitter-patter of rain is on the outside and you are on the in.

My reverie was interrupted by a horrible, truncated cawing, something guttural, like a crow with laryngitis. I lay there on the bench, my eyes scrunched against the sun, scanning the branches of the pines and the birches looking for the culprit. The short barks could have come from a Jack Russell terrier being strangled by a too-tight collar.

The perpetrator, a grey squirrel, sat thirty feet up in the pine tree at the other side of the garden on the junction of a bough and the main trunk. It was waving its tail like the official at a Formula One motor race waves his flag when warning the drivers of an accident on the track. I don't think the squirrel knew much about motor racing or black and white chequered flags, but it certainly knew about the black and white cat walking along the garden wall below the squirrel's perch. The squirrel was warning all of its grey brethren within hearing distance that a predator was on the prowl. The cat went on its way with an air of disdain, bordering on contempt, at the squirrely cacophony above.

The grey squirrel, *Sciurus carolinensis,* is an American beast, as the second part of its scientific name suggests. Its genus, *Sciurus,* comes from two Greek words, 'skia' and 'oura', meaning 'shadow' and 'tail', alluding to its habit of sitting in the shade of its tail.

Communication in the grey squirrel world is a lot more complex than you would imagine. It involves both sounds and postures, and can vary depending on where the squirrel lives: they have local accents like us. In open areas prone to noise pollution, such as a cityscape with traffic noise, squirrels are more apt to use visual signalling. Where the foliage is dense and vision is restricted, squirrels tend to vocalise more. Nobody has apparently told the noisy squirrels which live in the Grange area of Edinburgh this information. The Grange is reasonably open and relatively quiet, so squirrels to the south of the Meadows should be less loud and rely more on sciurine semaphore.

In the Journal of Mammalogy (November, 1984), Robert S. Lishak of the Department of Zoology-Entomology, Auburn University, Alabama, published a paper called *'Alarm Vocalizations of Adult Gray Squirrels'*. He describes the squirrels' four different alarm calls in a beautifully onomatopoeic manner, calling them a buzz, kuk, quaa and moan, all of which can be emitted in either pure or mixed sequences, or as one-note calls. He investigated 5000 vocalisations from 82 squirrels during 55 recording sessions.

Tail-swishing can be quite cute, but these endearing swishes are another means of squirrel communication, the import of which is hard to elucidate: tails can twitch, sending a wave along the tail like a slow-motion whip; and tails can wave just like the car-racing official's flag, in a figure-of-eight, a circle or an arc.

I'm left with the simple conclusion that squirrels are a lot more garrulous than would first appear. Should this be a surprise, given that the squirrel is such a successful, social animal? Probably not.

Still lying in the siesta-seat contemplating squirrel communiqués, again I was diverted by a sound from above. This time it was a big, black bird, flying with a slow beat, in the direction of Arthur's seat and Salisbury Crags, the hills which dominate Edinburgh's skyline and bring much character to Scotland's capital city. The bird's croaky squawk was fairly high-pitched for such a big bird and I thought it could be a raven, *Corvus corax*. Perhaps distance and perspective were playing with me and the bird was a smaller member of the *Corvus* genus. Ravens have been seen on Arthur's Seat within the last decade, and Arthur's Seat is only two miles away......as the crow flies.

October 13th

The nice people at Volkswagen sent us a letter telling us that our Skoda Yeti diesel car will need to have a software update. Its engine is one of eleven million across the world which has an engine control unit, its onboard computer, which cheats during emissions tests.

This software has been called a defeat device. It has the ability to detect when the engine is being tested for polluting emissions, then kicks in to alter the way the engine functions so that the vehicle passes the emissions test. After the test, during normal driving, the engine control unit switches off the control software to get better fuel economy and more power. This can result in up to **FORTY** times as much pollution as is allowed in law, according to website, www.consumerreports.org, in an article called, '*VW, Audi Cited by EPA for Cheating on Diesel Emissions Tests*', by Jon Linkov.

I am turning into Victor Meldrew, the grumpy, old curmudgeon from the situation comedy, *'One Foot in the Grave'*. His catchphrases sum up my mood: 'I don't believe it!' not actually said that often by old Victor, despite popular belief; 'In the name of sanity', heard more often; and 'Unbe-lieeevable', but sadly, not unbelievable. Volkswagen paid a $120,000 fine in 1974 over the use of defeat devices which disabled pollution control systems; they have a track record, and I don't mean a racing-track record.

It's often been said that history repeats itself; Mark Twain demonstrated his renowned insight when he wrote, 'a favourite theory of mine—to wit, that no *occurrence* is sole and solitary, but is merely a repetition of a thing which has happened before, and perhaps often.'

Which car company can you now trust?

Volkswagen has misled customers and governments in their attempts to increase revenue and market share through their deception, and they have played on peoples' environmental ethics and sentiments. But has their duplicity had any particularly disastrous, environmental effect?

The United States Environmental Protection Agency accused Volkswagen of being in violation of the Clean Air Act with respect to circumventing regulations with regard to NO_X emissions. NO_X is the general molecular formula for nitrogen oxides where X is a number which gives the ratio of oxygen atoms to one nitrogen atom in a particular oxide. The oxide of main concern is nitrogen dioxide, NO_2.

Michael Le Page explains this beautifully in *'Invisible Killer'*, an article in New Scientist (October 29th, 2016). Diesel vehicles are the biggest source of NO_2 and there is ample evidence that NO_2 has many harmful effects: it decreases weight at birth; it inhibits the growth of children's lungs; it increases the chance of respiratory infections; and it increases risk of cardiovascular disease. Statistics gurus suggest that NO_2 is responsible for the deaths of ten thousand people in the United Kingdom every year. That's the number that there is evidence for, but there may be many more deaths for which the evidence is yet to be discovered.

Volkswagen's and its associated companies' disgrace and dishonour have shown that despite modern cars having wonderful gadgetry and technology, they are still nowhere near as clean as they should be. *'Vorsprung durch Technik'* translates as *'progress through technology'* and, in the 1980s, was the uber-cool catchphrase used to promote Volkswagen's Audi brand of car. This slogan which once signified and dignified German technical expertise now rings rather hollow, with more than a hint of societal and customer betrayal.

October 14th

Just as the viburnums give the garden an autumn flower show at head height and higher, the lower borders glow in the sun with the scarlet delight that is the Crimson Flag, the African lily, sometimes still called the Kaffir lily. This last name is out of fashion and rightly so, given that it is an inappropriate anachronism from a colonial past and the K-word is judged as hate speech in the new South Africa.

The Crimson Flag is a wonderful late-season plant which flowers from late summer to early winter, depending on how sunny and protected is its site. Its two-inch, star-shaped flowers need direct sun to open fully. Up to ten flowers can develop on two-foot stems, looking great against the backdrop of their sword-shaped leaves. When I first grew these beautiful plants, the botanical name of this flower was *Schizostylis coccinea,* and to understand the derivation of *Schizostylis,* you need to know a little about a flower's female parts.

The pistil is the female part of the flower, made up of the stigma, style, and ovary. The stigma is the sticky bit in the centre of the flower on which pollen grains are deposited to then germinate and bring about fertilisation. The style is the stalk on which the stigma sits, connecting the stigma to the ovary. The ovary, usually at the bottom of the flower, has ovules inside that become seeds when fertilised. After fertilisation, the ovary develops into the plant's fruit.

So to the derivation of the name, *Schizostylis coccinea: Schizostylus* means 'split style' from the Greek, 'schizo', to 'cut' or 'split': which also gives us 'schism', a separation, usually religious; 'schizophrenic', as in split personality; and 'schist', a rock, the layers of which can be split. The style of *Schizostylus* is split in three. *Coccinea* means 'scarlet-coloured' and comes from the same root that gives us 'cochineal', the red dye.

Just as DNA data can convict criminals or clear the innocent, it can also be used to clarify taxonomy, the branch of science concerned with the classification of organisms, a practical and intellectual study which I am happy to leave to those who are more fastidious then me. *Schizostylus* doesn't deserve its own genus as its DNA is indistinguishable from that of the genus *Hesperantha.* In 1996, *Schizostylis coccinea* became *Hesperantha coccinea,* but gardeners being gardeners, old names tend to stick. Once you have learned how to pronounce and spell *Schizostylus*, and it being so appropriately named with its split style, why would you want to change what you call it? I'd go even further!

Hesperantha means 'evening flower'. *Schizostylis* is no evening-flower: it's a middle-of-the-day, I-like-being-in-full-sun flower, and it shuts up shop (and petals) not long after the sun has passed through its zenith. For me, this flower will continue to be *Schizostylis*, but don't tell the taxonomists.

October 18th

There has been some heavy rain over the last few days and the colder ground has retained the moisture. There's a real autumnal feel to the air now as the temperature drop has resulted in heavy, morning dew. The yellow birch leaves are scattered over the grass like golden confetti, leaving the birch branches bare and the cackling magpies, normally hiding in the foliage, easily seen in all their black-and-white magnificence.

I wandered the grass wondering whether to rake up the birch leaves, difficult though this is due to their small size, or should I wait for the westerly wind, common for most of the year but particularly so during

October and November, to dry off the leaves and blow them into convenient piles next to the wall.

Across the green, I spotted small golden-yellow orbs which, at a few metres away, I had taken to be leaves, but were, on closer examination, fungi. And the more I looked, the more I found, globes of citronella candle wax extruded through the turf, none larger in diameter than good-sized grape. By consulting my fungi books, I identified the mushroom as probably (all my fungal identifications are, at the very best, probable, and normally just maybes) the Butter Waxcap, *Hygrocybe ceracea.* Confirmation of the mushroom's probable identity was gleaned from my favourite mushroom website (www.first-nature.com). Pat O'Reilly and his wife Sue have produced this thing of beauty, an intellectual enchantment, when once discovered, it will hold you spellbound. When you thought you would have a quick look to confirm some aspect of anything from fungi to fly-fishing, you will while away an hour without even noticing the time pass. This website has made the list of websites which have enhanced my life. Visit it and enhance yours.

The name of the Butter Waxcap, *Hygrocybe ceracea,* describes the mushroom well, both its colour and texture. The cap has a greasy look and the colour becomes less golden and more the yellow of traditional butter as the toadstool ages. Butters which I buy these days appear to me rather pallid, and I wonder if there is some aspect of false memory or nostalgia which causes me to remember my childhood butter as yellow. *Hygrocybe* means 'wet head' and *ceracea* means 'waxy'.

If the thought of bodily secretions upset you, ignore the next two sentences and proceed directly to the next paragraph. The orangey-yellow to pale yellow transition which the mushroom undergoes brings to mind the various shades of assorted ear waxes. If you have had children, you may have managed to forget the diverse colours of your children's ear wax, and the pride with which your children took in presenting the stuff for your inspection.

Amongst the many yellow patches of mushrooms, one small patch was orange, with bits of the caps almost red, and it may have been *Hygrocybe coccinea*, the Scarlet Waxcap. On the other hand it could have been a *Hygrocybe ceracea* that had been affected by something in its environment such as a lack, or an excess, of a particular chemical.

These fungi like low-nutrient, mossy grass and appear with other members of their *Hygrocybe* genus. I stopped treating the back grass with moss-killer a few years ago and have since been rewarded with a much richer display of mushrooms and toadstools. The difference between mushrooms and toadstools is rather pedantic and depends very much on your taste, literally. Mushrooms are meant to be edible and toadstools are poisonous. It is advisable to consider all possible mushrooms as toadstools unless you are an expert in mushroom identification.

Encouraged by my success in finding my waxcaps, I looked more closely between the fallen birch leaves to discover a multitude of small, insignificant, brown toadstools, standing on skinny stems a few centimetres tall. They wore conical caps a centimetre or two, both high and wide. The central nipple on top of the cap gave the game away and name away as the Liberty Cap, or Magic Mushroom, *Psilocybe semilanceata,* a mushroom which contains the psychoactive substances psilocin and its phosphate ester, psilocybin. These chemicals are en*theo*gens, meaning 'generating the divine within'. They are chemical substances used in spiritual or religious circumstances which induce a psychotropic effect. The Mexican Liberty Cap, *Psilocybe mexicana,* looks very similar to its European cousin and has been used in religious ceremonies in Central and North America for over 2000 years. The Aztecs called this mushroom Teonanacatl, the 'god-mushroom'.

Psilocybin and psilocin, along with heroin and cocaine, are considered Class A drugs in the United Kingdom, and the use or possession of

Psilocybe semilanceata, or any other mushroom of that genus which contains these drugs, is prohibited. They may get you high or they may get you arrested so leave your small, brown mushrooms with the nipple on top to grow undisturbed on your lawn. *Psilocybe* means 'smooth head' and *semilanceata* means 'half spear-shaped', the conical mushroom head resembling a spearhead and the stem resembling the shaft. Well, they would resemble that if you had sampled a few of these mushrooms, I suppose. Seriously, however, do not eat these mushrooms because they can have a very negative effect on some people, inducing anxiety attacks, pain and vomiting: you could have a 'bad trip' and it could be a bad trip straight to your local Accident and Emergency.

It's not all negative. Psilocybin probably has a future in medical treatments as the title of an article, by Stephen Ross et al, in the Journal of Psychopharmacology (November 30th, 2016) indicates: *'Rapid and sustained symptom reduction following psilocybin treatment for anxiety and depression in patients with life-threatening cancer: a randomized controlled trial'.* The title of the paper is self-explanatory.

October 19th

Further foraging around the grass has resulted in the discovery of more wee, brown mushrooms, but lacking the Magic Mushroom's nipple. These proved to be the very common Brown Mottlegill or Mower's Mushroom, *Panaeolina foenisecii*. The common name, Mower's Mushroom, alludes to the fungus's predilection for well-mown lawns, so long as they are free of synthetic chemicals. This mushroom has a zoned cap with a dark band round the margin which fades when it dries, and which then darkens again if it gets wet; it is hygrophanous. It changes colour as it loses or gains water, so any such mushroom is difficult to identify from pictures of single specimens. *Panaeolina* means 'variegated and small', and *foenisecii,* 'foenus' is 'hay' and 'sec' is dry so the combination can be interpreted as associated with 'haymaking'.

If these names stir romantic imaginings of hayfields and John Constable's paintings, be aware that this cute, little, brown toadstool also contains psilocybin, so if you pick one, you are technically breaking the law. Mower's Mushrooms also contain the neurotransmitter, serotonin, thought to generate feelings of happiness. But don't be tempted: any mushroom can be difficult to identify and as I'm no mycologist, I stick to my principle of not putting anything in my mouth unless I know what it is and where it's been.

October 20th

The fine, clear weather has been holding so it has been easy to keep motivated to do my daily constitutional walk around the block. It's about three quarters of a mile with mild slopes. I concentrate on my gait to retrain neuromuscular pathways and, on different days, I walk at different speeds, so different types of muscle fibre get a workout. The gait is probably more important than the speed because neuromuscular paths take longer to retrain than muscle fibres. The question which could be asked is why are neuromuscular paths important?

We have an innate awareness of where our different body parts are positioned and the angles at which these parts are aligned, even when we cannot see or feel them. The subconscious perception of our body's orientation and movement is called proprioception. This aspect of consciousness is supplied by the vestibular system in the inner ear and by nerves in our muscles and joints. It's the system that lets us know where our hands and feet are when we are blindfolded, even if we are waving our arms and legs around. You can always find certain bits of your anatomy quickly in the dark.

Proprioception, sometimes referred to as muscle-memory, is learned through experience, but can be compromised by changes in body-structure due to injury, aging or adolescence. Teenagers who go through a growth spurt may start to drop rugby and cricket balls which they used to catch. Their arms are now longer than their brain remembers. Adolescents' muscle-memory lags behind their growing bodies and the hands attempting to catch a ball are an inch longer from where they would have been six months ago, but the brain has not yet had enough time to learn this.

However, neuromuscular pathways can be retrained with specific practice: juggling helps cricketers. Movement and awareness exercise, such as tai chi or yoga, not only improves proprioception, but diminishes the likelihood of the falls and broken bones that are the bane of the elderly.

My right knee is now about four inches nearer my central axis than it used to be before my knee-replacement operation. In other words, my once-bandy right leg is now straight and certain muscles now pull at slightly different angles than previously. Some of these muscles are slightly more stretched and some slightly shorter. Calf, quadriceps, hamstring, butt and base of the back muscles all require time and effort to be retrained in their subtly altered tasks. Why should this be important to someone who has had arthritic knees and bandy legs?

Pre-operation, when my feet were together, my thighs would angle outwards leaving a six-inch gap between my knees. Post-operation, when my right thigh is at that same angle, my right foot is around three inches further to the right than it used to be. When walking on uneven ground, my old proprioception still tells me that my right foot is three inches to the left of where it is now in reality, and I have already experienced tumbles for that very reason. I have missed my footing several times in the garden. However, I am lucky: I understand why this happens and I know how this situation can be rectified, and that involves re-educating my neuromuscular pathways;

and I must be patient, as proprioception has a long and stubborn memory.

October 21st

Tranquil blue skies and light winds, so instead of the round-the-block walk, I strolled through the Marchmont area of Edinburgh to the Meadows, a large park to the south of Edinburgh Castle and the town centre. It comprises mostly of open grass with fine avenues of mature trees. The Meadows was, once upon a time, a loch, the South Loch, and before that it was called the Burgh Loch. Up until the early seventeenth century, this loch supplied much of the drinking water for the city's populace. The trees were my objective; I wanted to see their colours.

Abscission is not a word, I think, which would come to mind when most people admire autumn's colour scheme up in the trees and down on the ground. Many folk could possibly have a reasonable guess as to what it means. It's derived from the same Latin route as scissors and incision: 'ab-' is 'away from' and 'scissio' is a 'cleaving' or 'cutting'; basically, 'a cutting away from' or 'a cutting off'. An abscission is the shedding of a part of an organism, like a leaf from a tree in autumn. But why do they do it?

Leaves aren't as tough as twigs and branches so they would freeze in winter. Any plant tissue which can't survive severe weather must be shed so the main body can conserve nutrients and water. The same is true for trees which must survive summer droughts as it is for trees in temperate areas as winter approaches. Trees in Scottish gardens, such as my James Grieve apple tree, will lose leaves in summer during very dry periods for exactly this same reason.

As autumn days get shorter, tree hormones trigger the formation of specialised cells at the base of the leaf stem to produce a separation, or abscission, layer. At the start of the abscission process, trees re-absorb nutrients from their leaves and store them in their roots. The culmination of abscission is when the leaf is fully separated from the tree's transport system which results in leaf fall, the beginning of another natural process, that of decomposition and nutrient recycling. Oak and beech are two of the deciduous trees which do not undergo full, autumnal abscission as they like to hang on to their leaves for most of the winter, especially those on branches nearer the ground, but more of that later.

It is this process of abscission which causes the autumnal palette of reds, oranges, yellows and browns that many of us love and look forward to, despite it heralding frosts and long nights.

Chlorophyll is the green pigment that gives leaves their spring and summer colour. Without chlorophyll, plants would be unable to capture sunlight and convert it into chemical energy. They store this energy in the form of carbohydrates (sugars and starch), through the chemical reaction called photosynthesis. Counter-intuitively, chlorophyll is not stable in strong sunlight so, during summer, it is constantly breaking down and being regenerated. Carotenoid compounds are also present. These are more stable chemicals, giving carrots and corn their orange and yellow colours. Chlorophyll and carotene colours combine to give leaves a light green shade if no other pigments are present, as is the case of birch trees and some species of poplar.

As days shorten and sunlight decreases, trees respond by producing less chlorophyll until they finally stop making the green compound, then the yellow and orange carotenoids shine through, giving us the golden showers of leaves from birches and Norway maples. As the chlorophyll breaks down and the breakdown products are transported out of the leaf, red pigments of anthocyanins can form. These act as a protective sunscreen to give extra time for excess nutrients to offload from the leaf before it falls from the tree. Anthocyanins give the reds and purples of Japanese maples, rowans and, of course, viburnums.

As a leaf-note, if carotenoids and anthocyanins are not present in autumn leaves, the leaves take on the grotty, brown colour of the detritus that is the dried, dead leaves under oak trees.

'October gave a party;
The leaves by hundreds came-
The Chestnuts, Oaks, and Maples,
And leaves of every name.
The Sunshine spread a carpet,
And everything was grand,
Miss Weather led the dancing,
Professor Wind the band.'

George Cooper (1840-1927)

October 23rd

Everybody seems to have a glut of apples this year and I can't give away my excess James Grieve crop. The southerly-facing walls that surround the gardens in the Grange provide ideal situations for apple-growing. Apple varieties which would be a bit too tender for Edinburgh's easterly clime seem quite happy when given the protection from wind by a wall and the bonus of the sun's heat radiated back to them from the stone behind. Hardier types of apple, like James Grieve, thrive, and it should come as no surprise that this apple is very common here in Edinburgh, its place of origin. James Grieve was a nurseryman, born in Peebles, who lived and worked in the Broughton area of Edinburgh. He produced this hybrid apple at the end of the nineteenth century from, it has been suggested, Cox's Orange Pippin and Potts Seedling.

The James Grieve apple is one of 7500 cultivars of the domesticated apple, *Malus pumila,* sometimes referred to as *Malus domestica.* Different cultivars are bred for different characteristics depending on whether the fruit is to be cooked, eaten raw or processed into juice or cider. Each cultivar may have its strong points, but also its weaknesses, such as lack of resistance to certain problems; fungal attack, bacterial assault and being specifically attractive to certain pests. Balance is sought by breeders when selecting parents for new cultivars, to enhance the positive and minimise the negative, surely a philosophy for every aspect of life.

James Grieve is the most wonderfully balanced apple in that it can be picked early before full ripeness and used successfully as a cooking apple, keeping its shape in tarts and crumbles. Picked a few weeks later when they are softer and sweeter, James Grieve apples retain a tangy, acidic sharpness which thick-skinned, hard-hearted, supermarket apples are surely jealous of, and these James Grieves have a delicate crispness, more akin to that of a firm pear than an apple.

The joy of the juice squishing from a sun-warmed James Grieve, as teeth bite the pale flesh of the apple plucked straight from the tree, is an experience which supermarket-apple eaters probably can't even imagine. To add to this, the James Grieve apple is a thing of aesthetic beauty: many red streaks adorn a yellow-orange skin which protects the flesh beneath. So why are they not found in the aisles of mediocrity, in the supermarkets from whence most of our sustenance is purchased?

That same gorgeous skin bruises easily, so James Grieve, despite its flavour, fell out of favour with commercial growers who require their fruits to remain blemish-free during transport. For me, the damaged fruits are eaten soonest, or juiced, while the undamaged can be stored for a few weeks. If excess apples are left on the tree to become overripe, wasps and birds will take their share, which is no bad thing.

As for James Grieve, the man, his grave is unmarked under a holly bush in Rosebank Cemetery by Broughton Road in Edinburgh. He lies close to where he lived and worked. It was found and photographed by Fay Young, a Broughton resident and writer, with a special interest in gardens and the environment. She tells the whole story of her sleuth-work and discovery in the Broughton History Society Newsletter, number 28. This can be found via Broughton's monthly community paper, The Spurtle, Broughton's independent stirrer.

For non-Scots and the uninformed, when I was a child, a spurtle was a wooden kitchen utensil used to stir porridge and chastise small boys who got too near the cooker. These modern days, a spurtle is a wooden kitchen implement used only to stir porridge, and small boys who remain unchastened may suffer serious burns. Each year, the World Porridge Making Champion is awarded with a Golden Spurtle at the Championship at Carrbridge, in the Cairngorm National Park.

Fay Young suggests that James Grieve's unmarked grave should be memorialised by the planting of an apple tree, at Plot 76, Section H in Rosebank Cemetery, to commemorate the great nurseryman. A specimen of *Malus domestica*, cultivar 'James Grieve', would be eminently appropriate.

October 26th

Yesterday, Lynn took the train from Waverly Station, Edinburgh to Dalmuir Station on the north of the River Clyde. She walked the ten minutes from the station to the Golden Jubilee National Hospital where she stayed overnight in the Beardmore Hotel, the hotel with conference centre attached to the hospital. The hospital was built in 1994 as a private hospital and the hotel was included to accommodate the relatives of rich, private patients. This entrepreneurial venture failed and was bought for the National Health Service to be the

National Waiting Times Centre to take referrals from across Scotland with the purpose of reducing patient waiting times.

The National Waiting Times Centre was a name which did not roll off the tongue well and carried too many negative connotations for politicians who oversaw the National Health Service in Scotland. Imagine implying that patients had to wait; so the centre was promptly renamed the Golden Jubilee National Hospital. The words 'golden' and 'jubilee' carry so much more positive import than 'waiting times': whoever came up with Golden Jubilee National Hospital will have certainly received a bonus or promotion for improvement to patient services.

Today, Lynn underwent hip replacement surgery. This is a reversal of roles. I have been looked after since my knee replacement two months ago and now I become the looker-afterer.

I drove along the M8 from Edinburgh to Glasgow, less than relaxed. As I got to Glasgow, my aim was the turn-off for the A814 which passes through Clydebank and Dalmuir, heading for Dumbarton. This road is referred to as the Dumbarton Road, or the Glasgow Road, depending on where you are on it and in which direction you are heading.

If I got to Dumbarton then I'd know that I had missed the Golden Jubilee turn-off. I did, however, find myself driving down Argyll Street in the middle of Glasgow, which was an indicator that I had missed a turn-off, the one for the A814. I realised that if I headed south for the River Clyde and turned right, westward, then I'd be heading in the correct direction. I did, and I was.

The weather was grey, dismal and dank, a depiction that also could have described me, if you had thrown in dejected and tired. Finding your way on a difficult road, one on which you have never travelled before, is both stressful and exhausting. Could 'getting through Glasgow' be a metaphor for dealing with life's travails?

Driving more or less parallel to the Clyde, finally heading west, I found that I was on the A816 Dumbarton Road, when I was overtaken, not by the police, but by a sense of relief, that feeling you get when you realise that you are not lost. At the same time, the low *Stratocumulus* cloud, which had been ominously looming overhead for the last half hour, broke slightly above the far bank on the south side of the Clyde, to create the most spectacular crepuscular rays.

Crepuscular rays are the sunbeams which form when sunlight breaks through gaps in the clouds, but are only apparent when defined by clouds' shadows. The rays are visible because dust, small water droplets and air itself scatter the light. If you are old enough to remember going to the cinema when smoking was allowed in these public places, you may recall, when you looked upwards, seeing the beam of light from projector to screen delineated sharply in the dark. This was caused by the smoke particles reflecting light downwards to your eye and the formation of crepuscular rays is much the same. Crepuscular rays are sometimes called God Rays, as the light breaking through the clouds appears to be leading from the earthly to the heavenly.

The word 'crepuscular' comes from the Latin for 'twilight' as these rays are more likely to be visible when the sun is low in the sky, at dusk and at dawn. They can be seen at any time of the day given the right clouds and suitable air conditions. If there is plenty of moisture in the air, but not enough to form a mist, then that moisture will scatter the sun's light. The shafts of sunlight brightened me and the day.

Lynn's surgery was successful and I stayed over in the Beardmore Hotel.

October 27th

There was some time to kill after breakfast before I was allowed to visit Lynn, so I took a circular walk through Dalmuir. This was an area about which I knew little and had never previously visited. The hospital and the hotel are attached back to back, so you can go from one to the other without getting wet. They sit together in massive grounds with copious parking at both the hospital side to the east and the hotel side to the west. I exited the building by the hotel side and walked through the car park and along the approach road to the west gate where I turned right on to Beardmore Road which led to the main Dumbarton-Glasgow highway, the A814, which I'd travelled the day before.

When I got to the junction of the two roads, there was a most fantastic work of art. The Beardmore Sculpture was created by local artist, Tom MacKendrick, and was commissioned by local residents' associations. The sculpture is built from sheet steel and is over thirty feet wide and high, surmounted by a magnificent, twenty foot model of the Revenge class battleship, HMS Ramillies, made of galvanised steel. This ship was laid down on the 12th November, 1913, at the Dalmuir Naval Construction Works, owned by William Beardmore, the site which is now occupied by the Golden Jubilee National Hospital and the Beardmore Hotel. At its acme, Beardmore's companies employed 40,000 people on Clydeside, 13,000 of whom would walk past this place where the Beardmore Sculpture now stands, on their way to their jobs in the Dalmuir Works.

HMS Ramillies saw action during World War 2 and played a major role during the Normandy landings where she successfully dealt with the Benerville battery of 6-inch guns. During the Normandy engagement, HMS Ramillies fired over a thousand 15-inch shells. No single ship had previously launched such a massive bombardment. She was scrapped in 1949, but one of her 15-inch guns was saved and can be seen at the Imperial War Museum in London.

Knowledge of William Beardmore and the Dalmuir Naval Construction Works allows you to appreciate how Dalmuir grew from a 'village with railway station', as described in the late 19th century by Frances Groome in *'Ordnance Gazetteer of Scotland'*: this can be viewed on the University of Portsmouth's website *'A Vision of Britain through Time'*. This vision of Britain, between 1801 and 2001, includes maps, statistical trends and historical descriptions (visionofbritain.org.uk). I now know a bit more about how Dalmuir grew and, sadly, how it declined through the 20th century, as did so much of our heavy industry.

I walked east along the Dumbarton-Glasgow road, the most obvious features being the CCTV cameras above the doors and TV satellite dishes on the walls of new flats, an expression of insularity and isolation in an area which was once a vibrant community and now lacked soul. This was made more depressing by the number of empty shops on the ground floors of the old tenements. The day and my mood were grey, the latter probably brought on through sleeping in a strange bed and my concern for Lynn, and it didn't improve as I trudged the quarter mile to the junction of the main road with Agamemnon Street, the road to the entrance at the hospital side of the Golden Jubilee complex. I turned right, past Benbow Road, in the direction of the hospital and the Clyde. You cannot avoid Dalmuir's naval history: HMS Agamemnon was involved in the Dardanelles Campaign and HMS Benbow participated in the Battle of Jutland.

The last half mile had blown the cobwebs away and maybe my breakfast was kicking in as I was feeling a bit more upbeat as I headed back to the hospital. This more positive mood was helped when I investigated the high-fenced land opposite Benbow Road, evidence that community spirit did survive and thrive in Dalmuir. Behind the secure fence was a set of garden allotments. These had been renovated in 2006 after the Dalmuir Plots Association had raised half a million pounds. I spent five minutes admiring the gardens and reading the information notices before moving on, back into the hospital grounds and across the huge car park to investigate the helipad, situated close to the embankment by the Clyde.

A big river is an awe-inspiring sight, especially when you get close to it. The helipad must have been no more than about thirty feet from the River Clyde and not ten feet above it. Thoughts of flooding went through my mind which, of course, shouldn't have been a surprise because, if you build on a flood plain, you have to expect the odd inundation.

I watched the river. Silent and powerful, the wide waters rolled past. The Clyde is ancient and has the aura of the preternatural: what has it witnessed over the millennia? I leaned on the fence by the helipad and looked up and down the Clyde, at its potency, at its potential, at its authoritative, empty silence. Once, thousands had worked here and the noise, deafening; thousands in overalls, jackets and flat caps, the smell of tobacco and the clanking and clatter of metal on metal. *'The hammer's ding-dong is the Song of the Clyde'* is a line in, *'Song of the Clyde'*, by R.Y. Bell and Ian Gourlay, and made famous by the Scottish tenor, Kenneth McKellar.

There is another Song of the Clyde worth investigation, a film in the British Film Council Collection. This film shows the pastoral Clyde in its upper reaches, Glasgow city when trams were king and Lower Clydeside in its docking heyday. You can watch it (film.britishcouncil.org/song-of-the-clyde) and see for yourself what has been and what has gone, and decide whether this is for the good or for the bad.

About a hundred yards from the helipad, towards the hospital is a memorial to the 6000, and upwards, who died on board the HMT (Hired Military Transport) Lancastria when it was sunk off the French port of St. Nazaire while taking part in the evacuation of British troops and nationals during Operation Ariel. They were being evacuated from France, two weeks after the Dunkirk evacuation.

No-one really knows how many died and estimates of the number aboard the ship ranged from 4000 to 9000 souls. The captain had been ordered to load as many evacuees as possible without regard to the limits set down under international law. This was the largest, single-ship loss of life in British maritime history, the lives lost greater than the combined loss of those who died in the sinkings of the RMS Lusitania and the RMS Titanic (RMS, Royal Mail Ship, denotes vessels under contract to the British Royal Mail).

News of the loss was suppressed in the interest public morale by the British Government, by order of Prime Minister Winston Churchill, because this tragedy occurred so soon after the Dunkirk evacuation. It is not difficult to understand why this decision was taken then; national leaders at difficult times must take difficult decisions. But this disaster has been exacerbated by being ignored, by being played down by government, for seven decades.

The reasons being any, or all, of the following: bureaucratic obfuscation; bumbling; thoughtlessness; mean-mindedness; lack of compassion; and a self-perpetuating, misplaced sense of loyalty from one set of bureaucrats to other sets of bureaucrats who have gone before and who should have made better decisions during their time. This seems to me to be nothing more than the face-saving of faceless bureaucrats by successive cohorts of the same, refusing to admit that errors may have been made in the past and ignoring such have compounded past misjudgements; shame on them all.

The Lancastria Survivors Association was set up after the war by Major Peter Petit, however this Association lapsed after Major Petit's death. The association was revived as the HMT Lancastria Association in 1980 with the purpose to remember and honour all those who were present or who lost their lives when the Lancastria was sunk.

For seventy years, the British Government refused to give the site of the Lancastria's wreck 'war grave' status. In 2005, they still refused because the site was in French territorial waters and so was outside the scope or the Protection of Military Remains Act 1986. The Ministry of Defence stated that such a move would be 'purely symbolic' and would have no effect, seemingly blind to the fact that symbolic gesture can have profound effects. After continued campaigning by the Lancastria Association and by survivors' relatives, documents, finally obtained under the Freedom of Information Act 2000, showed that it was possible that the site could be declared a 'war grave', despite the government's earlier protestations.

In 2015, the Ministry of Defence (MoD) stated that

> '....as the French Government has provided an appropriate level of protection to the Lancastria through French law and it is formally considered a military maritime grave by the MoD, we believe that the wreck has the formal status and protection it deserves.'

The wreck now lies about five miles from the French coastal town of St Nazaire in about 20 metres of water. The French Government, in 2006, decided to give the wreck special protected status, preventing any diving within 200 metres.

The Scottish Government, in 2008, issued the HMT Lancastria Commemorative Medal to commemorate those who died during the Lancastria disaster and those who survived it. The then Scottish First Minister, Alex Salmond, presented the first batch of the medals to survivors and to relatives of victims and survivors who have since died. On the back of the medal, an inscription reads,

> 'In recognition of the ultimate sacrifice of the 4000 victims of Britain's worst ever maritime disaster and the endurance of survivors – We will remember them'.

The front of the medal shows a depiction of the Lancastria with the words

'HMT Lancastria – 17th June 1940'.

The medal was designed by Mark Hirst, the grandson of Walter Hirst, who survived the tragedy. Survivors, the families of survivors and the families of victims have suffered a lack of recognition of this tragedy from a succession of British Governments.

Alex Salmond unveiled the Lancastria Memorial in the grounds of the Golden Jubilee Hospital in 2011, at the site of William Beardmore's Dalmuir shipyard, where the Lancastria was built. The memorial is a bronze sculpture, set on granite. It was created by artist Marion Smith from Fife. The bronze represents the early steel sheet construction of the Lancastria and was developed from original drawings for the construction of the Lancastria. If you are unlikely to visit the Golden Jubilee Hospital any time soon, you can still view pictures of the wonderful Lancastria Memorial (marionsmithsculptor.co.uk/commissions/lancastria-memorial). If you do visit the Golden Jubilee Hospital, and are able, find the memorial between the hospital building and the River Clyde.

The resilience and fortitude of the HMT Lancastria Association is to be commended.

I left the memorial behind and found Lynn in good spirits.

I departed from Dalmuir and the Golden Jubilee National Hospital, hoping for an uneventful journey back to Edinburgh, but no such luck. Another missed exit and I found myself driving under the Clyde, heading south, and visiting Govan for the first time in my life. Hitting the M8, I turned east, knowing that if the setting sun was at my back, I'd get to Edinburgh some time before dark.

October 28th

Lynn returned home, chauffeured by our younger daughter, Rebecca, who had been visiting her mother, knowing that she might have a passenger on the return journey to Edinburgh. She had no navigation mishaps. Maybe there is something to be said for IT devices that can tell you which roads to follow, IT devices which I refuse to use; we do have maps, after all. It is just a shame that my map-reading skills may leave a little to be desired.

The boot is on the other foot; Lynn's. After my knee operation two months ago, Lynn was chief carer, bottle-washer and go-for. These are now my tasks; let's hope that I live up to expectations. I had bought Lynn a reception-desk bell as a little, home-coming present so that she could summon assistance right readily if required. This may have been a mistake.

October 30th

Things are calmer in the household. It's gone lunchtime and Lynn is resting. So am I. I'm lying on the siesta-seat looking at a cerulean sky, a shade halfway between blue and cyan. The blue today is a pitch-blue, akin to pitch-black, it has depth, and looking into that depth, it is impossible to focus as the emptiness has no bird or cloud for perspective. It made me quite dizzy, so it was as well that I was lying down. Dizziness can be quite pleasant if you are lying down.

A jet-plane interrupted my musing. So small and so far, it must have been somewhere between thirty and forty thousand feet up, the cruising height for commercial airliners. It left a contrail which lasted for around two seconds as it gradually dissipated and disappeared. As the jet crossed the sky, it came to an angle at which the sun caught the plane and its contrail to shine like a slow-motion shooting star traversing the blue. The brilliance of the aircraft faded and the exhaust dimmed to beautiful-white before both disappeared behind a neighbour's grey, slate roof. I was tranquil. Perhaps the release from the tension and worry of the last few days was allowing me to relax. But then again, I was still taking strong pain-killers when I got tired and achy, and this last week had certainly been tiring and also a little achy.

'Contrail' is short for condensation trail, the tail that's left behind from an aeroplane's exhaust, and it can be used to predict the weather. Some folk call them vapour trails. They are man-made *Cirrus* clouds, as implied by their own Latin moniker, *Cirrus homogenitus.*

Plane fuel is hydrocarbon in nature, just like the petrol or diesel in your cars, so when it burns, as long as there is enough oxygen around, it creates water and carbon dioxide waste products. When the hot gases leave the engine, the water vapour cools and condenses to make tiny droplets, just like your breath when you exhale on a cold day to make the misty cloud we call steam. Unlike your misty breath, the water droplets from the exhaust quickly freeze to form ice crystals because it is very cold at 30,000 feet; the temperature could be minus 50°C.

Observant people will have noticed the mist that makes a contrail does not start immediately behind the plane, but around a plane's length behind it. It takes that time for the invisible water vapour, which exits the exhaust at a temperature of several hundred degrees Celsius, to cool and condense, before becoming visible. You can see a similar thing at the spout of a kettle. Most people see steam clouds coming out of a kettle. Few notice the invisible inch of water vapour at the kettle's spout before it cools to make steam.

I can predict that the weather will be settled with little change for the next couple of days. How can this be foretold, is it magic? No, it is because the contrail at the rear of the plane was short and quickly disappeared.

This means that the ice crystals which formed the contrail have evaporated, or more correctly, the ice crystals have sublimated, the term used when a solid changes directly to gas. If a contrail fades quickly, as it did today, the air mass through which the plane was flying is dry. This causes the contrail to dissipate quickly and such conditions at jet-plane altitude are indicators that the weather will remain calm and consistent.

If contrails persist, or worse, if they spread, the air must be moist and is probably unstable at that height, forewarning that there is rain to come, the next day or soon after. But be wary of predicting the future and note that clever and successful weather forecasters never commit to exactitude; so they can never be wrong.

How lucky we are to have contrails to help us prophesy the weather. Before the First World War, there were no contrails. It wasn't until after the Wright Brothers got their feet off the ground and first achieved the feat of powered flight in 1903 that contrails were possible. During the First World War, planes fuelled with hydrocarbons, flew higher into the cold air and their exhausts produced the earliest condensation trails, a novel and beautiful sight, high above the hell below.

November

'November always seemed to me the Norway of the year.'

Emily Dickinson (1830-1886)

'Most people, early in November, take last looks at their gardens, and are then prepared to

ignore them until the spring.

I am quite sure that a garden doesn't like to be ignored like this. It doesn't like to be covered

in dust sheets, as though

it were an old room which you had shut up during the winter. Especially since a garden

knows how gay and delightful

it can be, even in the very frozen heart of the winter, if you only give it a chance.'

Beverley Nichols (1898-1983)

'The thinnest yellow light of November is more warming and exhilarating than any wine they

tell of.

The mite which November contributes becomes equal in value to the bounty of July.'

Henry David Thoreau (1817-1862)

November 1st

It's All Saints' Day and the fine weather intimated by the disappearing contrail has so far lasted three days. These fine days at this time of the year mean cold nights and damp grass that sparkles with morning dew, with the scents and sense of gentle decay pervading the air and chill. I can walk backwards and exhale my own condensation trail and watch it spread and dissipate. As I ambled in reverse clockwise round the garden and under the wide overhanging branches of the pine tree, I created my own miniature crepuscular rays. Clouds of my steamy breath caught the sun, with the exhalations in the shadow of boughs and branches almost invisible.

Passing the Guelder rose, my contemplation on autumnal odours was brought up short as it was made fragrantly clear that a fox had spent the night nestled under the bush. Fox stink is not to be sniffed at. Olfaction is an important means of communication for most canids and especially our own red fox, *Vulpes vulpes,* from the Latin for 'fox'. Foxes have anal sacs which act as fermentation chambers where bacteria convert sebum into stinky secretions which can be left as calling cards. Skip the rest of today's musings if reading about smelly oozings makes you feel queasy.

Eric S. Albone and Truls O. Gronneberg, from the Department of Animal Husbandry and the Organic Geochemistry Unit, School of Chemistry, University of Bristol, had a paper published in the Journal of Lipid Research (Volume 18, 1977), called *'Lipids of the anal sac secretions of the red fox, Vulpes vulpes, and of the lion, Panthera leo.'* Lipids are fatty chemicals.

The authors wrote in their introduction that the major lipid constituents of fox anal sac secretions were fatty acids. This paper can be found on the web, so if you are interested in lions' anal glands you can look for yourself. I'm sticking to the subject of foxes, but I'll give you a flavour of how academic scientists will go that extra mile, which few would wish to travel, in their endeavours to extend the frontiers of knowledge. Given that I have previously suggested that you may wish to avoid this section, perhaps you are already asking yourself the question, how did Eric and Truls get their secretion samples from the foxes' anal sacs? This is your last chance to dodge the answer.

The answer is to be found in the 'Materials and Methods' section of the paper:

> 'Red fox anal sac secretion samples were obtained without sedation from untamed captive animals, raised in captivity, by using external digital pressure and directing jets of secretion from the two sacs into a collecting vessel.'

Respect to Eric and Truls, unless, of course, they got a technician or a naïve and ambitious undergraduate to do the job for them.

Fox urine also contains stinky, volatile chemicals, some of which are organic, sulphur compounds, renowned in chemistry to be some of the smelliest chemicals on the planet. The dog fox can quite clearly announce his presence to local vixens because dog-fox urine contains quinaldine, whereas vixen urine doesn't. Quinaldine will tell other males to get lost or there will be trouble, and it also informs females that there is a potential mate in the area who would like to get together with her if she is receptive.

Foxes use their scent glands (sounds so much nicer than anal sacs), faeces and urine to 'scent mark', to communicate with other foxes that they are in the locale, to advertise the extent of their territory and, if the scent-producer is female, to broadcast whether or not she is fertile. Many is the time I've cursed the fox which left a faecal deposit, high but not dry, on garden furniture or on the top of low walls, for all to see and sniff. This practice is not to deliberately annoy gardeners but is a way of announcing a fox's presence to all other foxes in the vicinity and to come, have a whiff and get the message. It's their form of social media; a sort of skitter-twitter.

November 3rd

It was 1964 when 'Jason and the Argonauts' came to Selkirk picture-house and I remember looking in the display window where photographs were used to advertise the forthcoming films. I'd be eight years old and the shots of skeletons battling bronzed, muscled heroes, and winged harpies attacking defenceless innocents stirred my imagination. The film lived up to my anticipation and there was the added bonus of the goddess, Hera, whom I thought was the epitome of the perfect woman. I don't think that I was alone in my fantasies. Honor Blackman, who played Hera, was also a star in the early Avengers series. She appeared in the James Bond film, Goldfinger, as Pussy Galore, the leader of a group of women aviators, Pussy Galore's Flying Circus, causing many young boys' fervid imaginings to loop-the-loop.

But back to Jason; the Golden Fleece was the objective of Jason's travels and travails. Hera explains that the fleece is to be found in the land of Colchis, now part of modern-day Georgia, by the shores of the Black Sea. Colchis is famous for its Naked Ladies.

A few doors up from where I live, I spotted Naked Ladies in a neighbour's garden. The first week in November is about the last week that you can expect to find Naked Ladies in shady corners of gardens in the Grange area of Edinburgh. I don't mean the good women of the capital, but the Autumn Crocuses, *Colchicum autumnale,* also called Meadow Saffron, Naked Ladies and also, in these days of gender equality, Naked Boys.

The Autumn Crocus, *Colchicum autumnale,* named from Colchis, its land of origin, is not a crocus at all but a member of the lily family. They are called Naked Ladies when they flower in the autumn because their leaves, which grow in the spring and summer, die back in the autumn and disappear leaving the crocus-like blooms naked to the October weather. If you have Autumn Crocuses in your garden, make sure that you can tell the difference between them and autumn-flowering members of the *Crocus* genus, for reasons which will become obvious. Members of the *Crocus* genus have three stamens compared with *Colchicum autumnale* which has six stamens.

The Royal Horticultural Society considers all parts of *Colchicum autumnale* to be highly toxic by ingestion. Don't go collecting pretty styles and stamens in the autumn to produce your own home-made saffron unless you can count stamens. The leaves of *Colchicum autumnale* grow at around the same time as, and are very similar to, the leaves of Wild Garlic, *Allium ursinum,* often referred to and picked as Ramsons.

There have been deaths. The Poison Garden Website (thepoisongarden.co.uk) reports and explains the circumstances and symptoms of five such deaths. If you have a macabre side to your character or have a general interest in phytotoxicology, the study of poisoning of humans and other animals by plants, then this is a website for you. It is beautifully presented, giving summaries, blog entries, videos, etymologies, dangers, incidents and folklore for most, if not almost all, of the poisonous plants to be found in the UK. There is a handy 'A to Z' link using the plants' botanical names, along with a common name 'A to Z' convertor to aid your navigation round this website. John Robertson, who runs this superb website, is to be highly praised.

All *Colchicum* species are poisonous containing alkaloids such as colchicine, but, like many poisons, colchicine, a powerful cell toxin, can be used therapeutically with precise dosage. It is used in the treatment of gout and against certain types of cancer. There are investigations into the efficacy of colchicine semisynthetics which may be as effective, or even more effective, than colchicine, but as they are not so toxic, side effects are less of a problem. Semisynthetics are compounds which are made by chemically altering naturally derived products. Morphine, a natural opiate, is an alkaloid found in the seedpod of certain poppy plants, but heroin, which is derived from morphine, is classified as a semisynthetic opiate.

Alkaloids are chemicals which contain a nitrogen atom as part of a ring of atoms in their molecular structure. Plants have evolved to produce alkaloids which serve as chemical defence weapons against animals which eat the plants, thus, alkaloids are highly toxic to animals, and that includes us. The main alkaloid in *Colchicum autumnale* is colchicine; the toxic dose of which is ten milligrams, while the lethal dose is forty milligrams. Best not to have anything to do with Naked Ladies in the Grange, or anywhere else for that matter.

November 5th

Just as Jason and the Argonauts fascinated me long ago, November 5th has also enthralled me and has continued to do so for decades. Squibs, fireworks, pyrotechnics, call them what you will; Catherine wheels, Roman candles, bangers and jumping Jacks, these were the things that small boys, and in my case, the adult with small-boy attitudes, looked forward to as November approached.

It has been a privilege to spend almost four decades being paid as a chemistry teacher, some days getting children to experiment with powdered metals burning and flashing in Bunsen burner flames, and watching pupils carefully introducing certain chemical compounds to the edge of the Bunsen flame to produce glorious colours.

Observing the wonder and awe on young faces when they sprinkled iron filings into a flame to sparkle and dance, or when they held a crystal of copper sulphate at the edge of the flame, turning the flame beautiful blues and glorious greens, it sometimes seemed bizarre that I was actually getting paid for having so much fun.

If there is anything that I miss now that I have retired, it is probably this. I console myself with the words of wisdom from Jim, also a retired teacher, 'your worst day retired is better than your best day working.' Some might think that such a view is a little cynical, but another way to look at it is that your future, if you are still working, can only get better. This is the power of positive cynicism.

A flock of ten long-tailed tits, *Aegithalos caudatus,* picked their way through the trees in the garden, acrobatically looking for insects and spiders in the nooks and crannies of the trees' bark. They are a quiet bird at this time of the year; but their gentle, thin, high-pitched seep-seep creeps into your awareness, and when you look up, you can feel rather than see their gentle movement. Like shy fairies, the birds process in an irregular, gentle, stretched-out string from branch to branch and from tree to tree. They are a lovely bird, but difficult to view in detail as they seldom sit still. Long-tailed tits appear black and white, but there is a delicate rose-pink which can only be spotted in good light, on their shoulders and on their under-parts. *Aegithalos* means 'titmouse with long tail feathers' and *caudatus* means 'tail', just to emphasise the point that this bird's tail is as long, or longer, than the rest of its body.

The reason that I like this bird so much is that until quite recently, they were uncommon in the Edinburgh area. My first sighting of a long-tailed tit was about five years ago, but now they are regular visitors to the garden and they always seem to bring their family and friends. The visiting flock of ten was probably related; parents, this year's fledglings and perhaps parents' siblings. Birds which fail to nest, or those which have had their nests raided by a predator, will assist a sibling. This behaviour is appositely called 'helping at the nest', but it also benefits the helpers, by increasing the chance that some of their genes, those shared with the fledglings' parents, are successfully passed on through the next generation.

Andrew McGowan, Ben J. Hatchwell and Richard J. W. Woodburn, writing in the Journal of Animal Ecology (2003, 72 (3): 491–99), in '*The effect of helping behaviour on the survival of juvenile and adult long-tailed tits, Aegithalos caudatus',* described the benefits of 'helping at the nest'. They found that failed breeders that became helpers had a higher survival rate than failed breeders that didn't become helpers. But all is not negative for non-helpers.

The authors also found that failed breeders which didn't become helpers had a higher chance of successfully breeding in a subsequent year compared to those failed breeders which did become helpers: there is more than one way to load the genetic dice when these dice are rolled in Nature's casino.

Is it too great a step to consider that some of the conclusions of Andrew McGowan and his fellow authors may help explain the generosity of benevolent, bachelor uncles and caring, spinster aunts towards ungrateful nieces and nephews?

November 6th

It's warm for the time of year, unseasonably so. This has benefits in that it gives an elongated growing season for brassicas and leeks. But even though it's mild, the ground retains dampness and rarely dries off as the low sun's rays hardly touch the garden as they dance through the bare branches of neighbours' trees. The east wall and the houses to the south of the back garden cast their lengthening shadows over the vegetable plots, encouraging rusts, moulds, liverworts and algae. The grass seems to be metamorphosing into moss, which appreciates the dank, damp and relative warmth, just as the fungi do, pushing their fruiting bodies through the moss layer and grass thatch, to enthral with their colours, shapes and attitude, almost defiant in their unabashed boldness.

The warmish damp brings with it, mist and fog. As warm, humid air crosses the cold North Sea to the east of Edinburgh, the air temperature drops and, as cold air cannot hold as much water vapour as warm air, ground-level cloud develops. Ground-level cloud is better known as mist, or fog. Depending on where you live, you may have your own name for ground-level cloud: haar, fret, rime, rouk and woor. Two of these I knew.

The other three, I discovered in *'Lights, hazes, mists and fogs'*, one of the seven sections of the Coastlands Glossary in Robert Macfarlane's book, *'Landmarks'*. In this lexical delight, Robert Macfarlane takes you on a tour of the UK's landscapes: flatlands, uplands, waterlands, coastlands, underlands, northlands, edgelands, earthlands and woodlands. On your journey, he introduces you to the language which these landscapes have generated, all the while keeping you close to multiple natures, the nature of the landscapes, the nature within the landscapes, the nature of language and the language of nature. Nature study has never been so good.

November 7th

Today I'm scoffing Pink Fir Apples. So what's a Pink Fir Apple?

It's not a fir and it's not an apple, but there are sometimes pink bits. What it is, is a potato, *Solanum tuberosum*. It's my favourite potato, a maincrop potato. Potatoes are categorised as early potatoes or maincrop potatoes depending on how long it takes them to develop to a size ready for harvest. First earlies can be ready in as little as 12 weeks from planting to eating; second earlies take a little longer from 14 to 16 weeks; and maincrop take from 16 to 24 weeks depending on the variety.

Pink Fir Apple takes about 22 weeks here in Edinburgh. Other gardeners can claim shorter maturation times depending on how sunny and moist their vegetable plot is and on how smugly competitive they are. By planting first earlies in the middle of March and second earlies and maincrops from the middle of April to the middle of May, depending on the weather, I can be eating my own potatoes from the end of June through to November, and perhaps even December if the maincrop yield is good.

There are few vegetables which you might wish to eat on their own, but potatoes which you have planted, grown, dug from the ground, washed and cooked are certainly a candidate for mono-cuisine. Steamed Pink Fir Apples with a smear of butter or a daub of mayonnaise hit the mark. They are a rare November treat, a waxy, maincrop potato that is as delicious cold as it is hot, with an almost nutty flavour. Leftovers from an evening meal seldom survive to the following day's lunch.

If you belong to that strange sect that insists on peeling potatoes, Pink Fir Apple is not for you. They are long and knobbly, which makes peeling them difficult, to say the least; a good scrubbing, leaving the brown-to-pink-to-purple skin intact, which is hardly noticed in the eating, is sufficient precooking preparation. The adjective knobbly hardly begins to describe the shape of Pink Fir Apples as you get knobs on the knobbly bits, with some potatoes able to stand on end and look decidedly rude.

Others can be quite aesthetic and dolphinesque. Another advantage is that they store well, that is, if you store them at all, because if friends have sampled your Pink Fir Apples, they will happily help you deplete potential stores.

These potatoes are not difficult to grow, but like many things, are difficult to grow well. Pink Fir Apple is a very late variety so it's better to start them a bit earlier than you normally would a maincrop: this gives them a longer growing season before the dreaded blight comes in. Another factor that needs taken into account is that their shaws (green parts above ground) can be up to seven feet long; long rather than tall because they fall over and intrude on whatever is growing next to them.

If the overt knobbliness of Pink Fir Apple potatoes puts you off then I can recommend its spawn, Anya, which was bred from Pink Fir Apple and another potato called Desiree. Anya has inherited qualities from both parents.

When I first grew Anya, a second early potato, I thought, like Pink Fir Apple, it was a heritage potato. I was surprised to discover that it had been bred as recently as 1996 at the Scottish Crop Research Institute and is grown solely for Sainsbury's supermarkets. The potato was named after Lord Sainsbury's wife, Anya. Despite Anya (the potato) being less knobbly than Pink Fir Apple, and almost as nutty, Lord Sainsbury must have been quite brave to have named a knobbly, nutty potato after his wife.

Before finishing this bit on Pink Fir Apple potatoes, something needs said about the rather idiosyncratic name. I have no evidence for the origin of the name but I'm willing to propose two hypotheses.

Pink Fir apple potatoes appeared in Europe, mainly in France and Germany, in the middle of the nineteenth century, parentage unknown. They made their way to Britain from either France or Germany or, most probably, both.

The first hypothesis involves French, and fairly obvious it is too. French for apple is 'pomme' and French for potato is 'pomme de terre'. Some gardeners or farmers, in the south of England, whose French left a little to be desired, could easily have confused 'rose sapin pomme' with 'rose sapin pomme de terre'; in French, 'rose' is 'pink' and 'sapin' is 'fir'.

This is my less favoured hypothesis. Given that some French folk refer to Pink Fir Apple potatoes as 'sapin rose pomme pomme de terre' would indicate to me that language as well as potatoes travelled in both directions across the Channel.

My favoured hypothesis is of German origin. Germans referred to these potatoes as 'Rosa Tannenzaphen' which translates directly as 'pink fir cones', which accurately describes the general shape of many of the potatoes. In some areas of Austria, the potato is still called 'Rosa Tannenzaphen'.

Imagine the farmers or gardeners from the south of England trying to get their minds and ears round the German language and intonation when these potatoes crossed the channel. Repeat 'Rosa Tannenzaphen' several times out loud to yourself, if you're in a room on your own; if there are others within hearing distance, it may be better to stay silent than be regarded as an idiot. With repetition, if the 'z' becomes softer, if the consonants a little indistinct and if Kent gardeners/farmers were a little deaf, 'Rosa Tannenzaphen' can easily become 'Rosa Tannenaphel', or 'Pink Fir Apple'.

With the peculiarities of pronunciation and perception, I don't think that it is too big a step to suggest that 'zaphen', in the context, could have been easily perceived as 'aphel', German for 'apple'. We'll probably never know.

November 8ᵗʰ

A gang of juvenile greenfinches have taken over the sunflower-seed bird-feeder, and a rumbustious lot they are. Not so hot in skill development, they have difficulty landing on the feeder-perches when compared with their rather more adept parents. These elders fly up and land, assume a dominant aspect, threatening with an open beak any fledgling daft enough to presume an adult would relinquish their parental, feeding privilege. When the adults flew off, a pair of rather scruffy youngsters gingerly landed on a perch either side of the feeder and took over the dominant role keeping other youngsters at bay.

Watching them eat was fascinating. They obviously enjoyed the sunflower seeds, but just as their flight skills were in need of development, so were their eating abilities. Whereas an adult would take a seed, manipulate it in their beak, spit out the husk and swallow the seed, the juveniles had husks and bits of seed stuck all over their chest feathers and face. One had a bit of something between its beak and its eye that was irritating it but lacked the coordination to remove it. The young greenfinches on the feeder resembled a couple of toddlers trying to eat mince and potatoes with their fingers; only a fraction of the food gets in the mouth and a lot ends up sticking to other assorted body parts.

Greenfinches are another organism which has undergone a name change in the light of DNA evidence. The greenfinch was previously *Carduelis chloris*, but DNA research showed that the *Carduelis* genus of the finch family was polyphyletic, from the Greek, 'of many races'. The greenfinches were moved to their own genus, *Chloris,* the Greek for 'green': also giving us chlorine, chlorophyll, chloroplasts and chlorotic.

Our UK greenfinches are now *Chloris chloris*, one of five species in the genus. That name would indicate that our species is the green greenfinch; which happens to have ten subspecies, one of which is called *Chloris chloris chlorotica.* Who'd be a taxonomist?

This brings me nicely back to toadstools. When the birds had flown, I crossed the grass to see what bits of the sunflower 'hearts', as the birdseed sellers call the kernels, had been getting spat out by the finches. I didn't get as far as the feeders as I was distracted by a group of golden-yellow mushrooms very much like the Butter Waxcap, *Hygrocybe ceracea,* which I'd seen a month earlier. This *Hygrocybe* had an orange-red tint in the middle of its cap. I identified it as the Golden Waxcap, *Hygrocybe chlorophana.* The 'Golden' part of the common name is very appropriate but the 'chloro' part of the scientific name is not, as you'll realise from the paragraph above, given that there is nothing green about it. It's still an incredibly cute toadstool, if toadstools can be cute.

Three steps further and there's more of the golden-yellow fungus but the caps have been knocked of leaving the stems, 4-5cm tall and 5mm in diameter, with little white tips where the caps had been, or so I thought.

Closer examination of the stems and the fungus books proved them to be a type of club fungus. Why? Because their stems look like mini-clubs. They were either the Yellow Club fungus, *Clavulinopsis helvola,* or the Apricot Club fungus, *Clavulinopsis luteoalba.* You apparently need a microscope to differentiate between them, *helvola* having spiny spores and *luteoalba* having smooth spores. 'Clava' is Latin for 'club', the kind you can bash people with: '*helvola*', means 'honey-yellow' and '*luteoalba*' means 'yellow white' pertaining to the yellow stem and white tip, so the more likely candidate for my club fungus. Who'd be a taxonomist?

November 11th

The toadstools are mushrooming, so to speak. In three days, two fairy rings of brown mushrooms, for which there had been no previous evidence, have suddenly appeared. They are the Fairy Ring Mushroom, or Fairy Ring Champignon, *Marasmius oreades,* and are particularly interesting for a number of reasons.

The genus, *Marasmius,* was named by the Swedish mycologist, Elias Magnus Fries, who classified white-spored agarics as *Marasmius* if they had the property of being able to dry out and wither, but later revive when moistened. Mushrooms possessing this property can be described as marcescent, as opposed to its opposite, putrescent, which describes most mushrooms; they rot, decay and decompose, they putrefy. Marcescent and *Marasmius* descend from the same Latin root, 'marcescere', meaning 'to dry out' or 'wither'.

Oreades or the Oreiades were, or are, depending on your beliefs and imagination, Greek nymphs of hills, groves and woodlands, places where these mushrooms might grow.

Fairy Ring Mushroom are edible and may have a certain sweetness, especially the caps, due to the presence of a disaccharide sugar called trehalose, which comprises of two monosaccharide glucose units joined together. It is suspected that it is the trehalose that imparts the marcescent properties.

I would not be tempted to pick Fairy Ring Mushrooms for food unless you are a tip-top fungal forager, as you could end up as a dead fungal forager. There are two of the genus, *Clitocybe,* meaning 'flattened-head', *Clitocybe dealbata* and *Clitocybe rivulosa,* which grow in the same areas as *Marasmius oreades* and can also form fairy rings. Many mycologists consider these two *Clitocybes* to be the same species, but whatever the case, beware. They are very poisonous, containing muscarine, and can be deadly to consumers with a weakened cardiovascular system.

Dealbata, from the Latin, 'dealbare', 'to whitewash', may describe more than just the colour of the mushroom: if you ate it, you could take on the appearance of being whitewashed yourself as the consumption of these *Clitocybes* brings on circulatory disorders within half an hour of eating.

Peter George and Narasimha Hegde, writing in Toxicology International (2013 Jan-Apr; 20(1): 113–115) in their paper, *'Muscarinic Toxicity among Family Members After Consumption of Mushrooms'* reported on four family members who had eaten *Clitocybe* mushrooms and developed muscarinic poisoning. Their symptoms sound horrendous:

'Systemic muscarinic manifestations such as exhaustion, irritability, muscular cramps, salivation, frothing from mouth, sweating, lacrimation, blurring of vision, miosis, ptosis, bronchorrhea, cough, wheeze, tachypnea, rhonchi, bradycardia, hypotension, abdominal cramps, vomiting, and diarrhea were observed…(sic)' in all four patients.

Sort of puts you off picking your own mushrooms?

The good news is that all four were out of hospital after two days, having been treated with the muscarine antidote, atropine, an alkaloid poison present in the nightshade family, including the deadly nightshade, *Atropa belladonna*; but more of atropine later.

November 15th

Almost all the remaining leaves have been cleared from the trees by Storm Abigail which, like most storms that blast the United Kingdom and Ireland, blew in from the west. This was not unusual other than for one aspect; it had a name.

The Met Office decided that to help raise awareness of severe weather and improve public safety during such storms, they would have a name. Someone in the Met Office obviously had a sense of humour in naming the first storm, a big gale. So Abigail came, and Abigail went, stripping all leaves that were left on the trees, other than the topmost leaves on the poplar next door. They have a hint of green about them even though the rest of the tree's leaves have gone. These leaves catch the last rays of the sun as it sets and the shadows of the houses climb the trees, leaving the tops last to say goodbye to the evening light. It's probably this late light that gives the top leaves their longevity compared to the rest. A tree's leaves next to street lights are slower to take on their autumn colours than the tree's leaves on the side away from the light.

The wet, yet mild, weather has encouraged even more mushrooms to push through the grass. Hundreds of small, brown toadstools with caps like helmets or hats are all over the grass and they all look slightly different from each other. They could be the same species or several different species. They probably belong to the *Mycena* or *Galerina* genera, the bonnet and helmet mushrooms, of which there are hundreds of species, and I wouldn't even consider trying to accurately identify them.

Small they may be, but they are not to be taken lightly. Many of the *Mycena* and *Galerina* species are poisonous, and *Galerina* species can contain a particularly nasty group of poisons called amatoxins which can be lethal even in small doses. What's worse is that amatoxins are not destroyed by heating like many other mycotoxins, so cooking these mushrooms does not diminish their danger. Leave small brown mushrooms well alone.

It's not only fungi that have been appreciating the clement November conditions. A 2mm midgie was using the back of my left hand as a snack bar. Two weeks previously, a rare third generation of midgies had been predicted for this year; two annual generations is the norm. My insect guest was duly squished, but not quickly enough: a 5mm diameter red blotch appeared ten minutes after the squishing. There is genetic variation in human reaction to insect bites, be it a midgie, berry bug or mosquito bite, and I was at the front of the queue when the genes were given out which cause a person to react badly to these bites (see September 4th).

November 16th

We were driving back into Edinburgh from the Bilston direction so we were heading more or less northeast. It was almost midday so the glorious autumnal sun was roughly at our backs and a high rainbow arched over Edinburgh, honouring Scotland's capital city. Within a few minutes, the squally showers, which had been reflecting the sun's rays and producing the rainbow, were being blown over the Forth estuary by a westerly wind. It's worth remembering that if you see a rainbow with the sun at your back and the wind is in your face, you'll soon be wet: if you see a rainbow with both the sun and wind at your back, you're wet already.

The wonderful optical phenomenon that is the rainbow has been arcing over the skies for as long as there has been simultaneous sunshine and rain. When might our hominin ancestors have first cast their eyes skyward and recognised the spectral bow as the aesthetic glory that it is? Which of these ancestors would have first perceived and appreciated beauty in the sweep of the rainbow's curve?

Australopithecus (4,000,000 years ago), *Homo habilus* (2,000,000 years ago), *Homo erectus* (1,000,000 years ago), *Homo neanderthalensis*, the Neanderthals (400,000 years ago), or was it only us, *Homo sapiens*, having evolved from archaic humans around 200,000 years ago who have gazed in wonder at rainbows. Neanderthals made elaborate tools, controlled fire, lived in complex social groups and fashioned jewellery from talons, animals' teeth, shells and ivory. They had language and created cave paintings.

Neanderthals, I believe, having had an appreciation of the artistic, would have had a word for, or at least some way to describe, a rainbow, and they would have been in awe at its beauty and magnificence: just as I was today. Maybe that's the few percent of the Neanderthal genome which is present in my genome, and yours.

As a Neanderthal sat by his fire, at the entrance to his cave, with the walls on which he has scratched his marks, napping a hand-axe, little could he know that his kind would become extinct. This could have been due to either interaction with modern-type hominins, or to natural catastrophic change, climatic, tectonic or pandemic. Whichever, I can still feel sadness for his loss. He was my ancestor and he is your ancestor. Most of us have inherited between 1% and

4% of our genetic material from Neanderthals, the hereditary legacy of interbreeding between Neanderthals and ancient humans. Over two decades playing rugby in the front row of the scrum has confirmed to me that there is a little Neanderthal in us all, more in some than in others.

Having knowledge of how a rainbow forms, and the science involved, makes its manifestation even more awesome. I use that word in its traditional meaning of 'breath-taking', not in the modern sense, where the word 'awesome' is overused and its meaning has been relegated to something more akin to 'quite nice'.

When you see a rainbow, there is a straight line between the sun, your eye and the centre of the circle of which the rainbow's arc is part, with its imagined extension hidden underground completing the ring.

If you don't have a real rainbow to look at, imagine the sun behind you and rain in front of you reflecting sunlight to produce a rainbow in your mind's eye. Now envisage all the ground in front of you disappearing so that you are standing on the edge of a precipice. The arc of your rainbow in the sky in front now extends to complete its circle below the level of your feet. The diameter of your circular rainbow subtends an angle of 84° at your eye, a little less than a right angle.

The raindrops which produce your rainbow are, at that instant, not at a particular distance away from you, but at any distance on the surface of the 84° cone that extends from your eye. Exactly the same rainbow is seen whether the raindrops are near you or far away, so unless you have something large behind your rainbow, such as a tree or a hill, it's very difficult to guess the height or distance from where the rainbow is materialising, where the rain is falling.

This is a primary rainbow, caused by light entering raindrops and being refracted (bent), then reflected from the back of the raindrop and refracted for a second time on leaving the drop to travel to your eye. The different colours of light are refracted by differing amounts, blue more and red less, resulting in the rainbow spectrum with red on the outside of your rainbow and blue on the inside. Sometimes a secondary rainbow can be seen outside the arc of the primary rainbow: and very occasionally, a third, tertiary rainbow can be observed beyond the secondary.

A secondary rainbow forms when light enters raindrops at such an angle that it is refracted once, then reflected twice internally before being refracted again on exiting the drop. This light forms a circular rainbow which subtends an angle of 104° at your eye, wider than a right angle. Its colours are reversed due to the double reflection, so the blue part of the spectrum is on the outside of the secondary rainbow and red is on the inside, the reverse of that of the primary rainbow. The secondary rainbow is also dimmer than the primary because the light is reflected twice, and some light is lost through the back of the raindrop on each reflection.

Three reflections are required for a tertiary rainbow which goes some way to explaining why they are so dim that they are difficult to observe, never mind that they are closer to the sun so this makes them even harder to see. If you are ever lucky enough to see a tertiary rainbow, or even a small part of one, and the ambient light is such that you can differentiate the colours, notice that the colour order is the same as the primary rainbow, with red on the outside and blue on the in.

People with an acute observational ability may have noticed that the sky inside the rainbow seems brighter than the sky outside its arc. This is more apparent with a double rainbow, because outside the secondary bow also seems bright, with a dim band between the two rainbows. Due to the refractive index of water, light coming from raindrops falling between the primary and secondary rainbows is not directed at the observer, but in other directions so the sky is less bright between the two rainbows. This dull band between the two rainbows

is known as Alexander's Dark Band after the Alexander of
Aphrodisias who described the phenomenon in 200 CE.

November 18th

After a dry September and October, November came in with westerly
winds and rain, Storm Abigail announcing her presence in no
uncertain wet and windy terms. Abigail has gone but some of the rain
which has followed in her wake has been of the very wet kind. The
wetting effect of some rain is certainly greater than others, depending
how heavy the rain is, wind speed, raindrop size and speed of raindrop
descent. The thing that got me thinking about this was that some
recent rain has been almost painful when hitting the head, so what
factors, on a still day, affect the pain-causing capacity of a raindrop
hitting a bald head?

There are two aspects of a raindrop which affect its energy and hence
how painful it feels when it hits. These are the size of the raindrop and
the speed at which it falls. The raindrop's size is limited to a
maximum diameter of around 5mm because, above this size, the force
of air-resistance, pushing against the drop as it falls, causes the droplet
to disintegrate making smaller raindrops.

The maximum speed at which a raindrop can fall, its terminal
velocity, is the speed at which the air resistance pushing upwards
against the raindrop equals the force of gravity pulling it downwards.
This speed is dictated by the raindrop's size.

The larger the raindrop, the higher is its terminal velocity. A 5mm
drop rapidly reaches its terminal velocity of around 9 metres per
second, or 20 miles per hour. This will vary slightly depending on the
temperature and humidity of the surrounding air. The height from
which a water droplet falls has no bearing on its pain-inducing energy

once you get higher than around twenty metres as this is the height required for a droplet to reach its terminal velocity.

A few years ago, when I still had to work for a living at Portobello High School, I persuaded a pal and fellow chemistry teacher, Michael, to join me in an investigation of falling raindrops, to see if we could compare the relative energies of different sized drops. I released 'raindrops' from a burette above Michael and Michael 'caught' them down below in a 'puddle', a water-filled container with a ruler taped to the side. I'd noticed, even as a child, that heavy rain would sometimes 'bounce' on a wet road surface, so the idea was that the height of the 'bounce', or recoil, of the 'raindrop' from the surface of the 'puddle' would give a relative measure of a droplet's energy.

The old Portobello High School had eight floors above ground level with narrow stairwells and minimal horizontal air movement, ideal for 'raindrop' investigations. The 'raindrops' were released from between the stair railing and down the stairwell to Michael below, who caught them in the 'puddle' and measured the 'bounce' against the ruler.

A 'raindrop' of 4mm diameter falling two floors into a 'puddle' produced a back-splash or 'bounce' of about 5cm. One falling four floors gave a 'bounce' of about 15cm and one falling six floors just over 20cm. Examining the difference in the height of the fall and the splash, the last splash may not be as large as you might expect, but this was no surprise because the droplets had probably reached their terminal velocity after falling from a height equivalent to about five floors.

A 4mm 'raindrop' falling six floors onto skin feels like being hit by a grain of rice dropped from a few metres. A 5mm 'raindrop' is almost twice as heavy as a 4mm drop because its volume is almost twice that of the 4mm drop (volume of a sphere = $4/3\pi r^3$), and the 5mm drop has a slightly greater terminal velocity. This results in a 5mm raindrop having roughly twice the energy of a 4mm raindrop and it is mildly painful when hitting a lightly-haired head from six floors.

Larger raindrops are possible but very unusual. The largest raindrops ever recorded were in Brazil in 2004 and measured up to a diameter of 10mm and would have had an energy of about eight times that of a 5mm diameter raindrop. Ouch!

Robert Macfarlane lists a hundred words or expressions associated with *'Rain and Storm'* in his book, *'Landmarks'* (see November 6th), but nowhere did I see any word or phrase which described how painful rain could be. Could 'prainful' denote the sensation experienced by bald heads in a downpour?

Pupils who witnessed this elaborate fandango on the stairs of the old Portobello High School looked at Michael and me as if we were mad. Perhaps so, but we were happy in our endeavours.

November 19th

The rain has abated, the wind has dropped and there are no leaves left on the *Viburnum*. The *Viburnum farreri* flowers are catching the November light slightly better than the *Viburnum bodnantense,* probably because the *farreri* is less pink and its white seems to glow. Some years, the *farreri* has held flowers from September until early May, the flowers looking like delicate, little pompoms at the ends of rigid, dark brown twigs, and their perfume is sublime.

Grow *Viburnum farreri* by a gate and enjoy its scent on winter's gloomy, depressing days. The fragrance is at its height in the late evening, which suggests that in its area of origin, its pollinators are likely to be moths or some other night-feeders looking for nectar, the sugary treat which flowers supply in payment for pollination. From late afternoon through until night, the darkness of winter is brightened by the superb bouquet of *Viburnum farreri.*

When days are shortening and chills are deepening, plants which flower when others do not are valuable mood-enhancers. A few feet away from the *Viburnum farreri*, there is a big clump of pink *Schizostylis* (*Hesperantha* to modernists) *coccinea*, which is probably the cultivar 'Sunrise', more delicate than the larger-flowered and more common, scarlet cultivar, 'Major'. Cultivar is one of these interesting portmanteau words, a word made up from a linguistic blend of bits of words. If you ate *brunch* today, you ate a portmanteau meal, combining *br*eakfast and l*unch,* which may have included a froghurt, a *fro*zen yo*ghurt,* not an amphibian upset at being eaten. *Cultivar* is a combination of *culti*vated and *vari*ety.

The 'Sunrise' *Schizostylis coccinea* has star-shaped, pink blossom which, if the sun is shining, gradually opens through morning and midday into the early afternoon. It starts to close its petals mid-afternoon, and shuts for the night; tendencies similar to my own at this time of year.

On less sunny days, when clouds finally break, and the racemes of flowers catch the November sun, *Schizostylis coccinea* 'Sunrise' greets the sun by opening wide its pink, six-petalled perfection to capture warmth and light, just like a small boy opens and spreads his arms wide to greet a favourite aunt, which warms her heart and brightens her day, just as *Schizostylis coccinea* 'Sunrise' does mine.

November 22nd

Yesterday, the wind came out the north and any leaves which had survived the earlier westerlies have flown on the breeze. Even next door's poplar is finally denuded, the apical leaves having, at last, learned the meaning of abscission (see October 21st). Some of the apical leaves, those at the top of the tree, were huge, ten inches long, not counting the stalk, and eight inches wide. It is a superb tree, but entirely unsuitable for the urban garden. An ex-neighbour planted it about fifteen years ago as a nostalgia-tree, because it reminded him of his time in North America.

He suggested that the tree was a Balsam Poplar, probably a Western Balsam Poplar, and this agrees with my own identification, *Populus trichocarpa,* also known as the Black Cottonwood. Its rate of growth is phenomenal, which I have witnessed; about two metres a year when it gets going, and this one now stands at about twenty five metres high. The then neighbour, Richard, knew the growth could possibly get out of hand but readily accepted the risk and that it may need cutting down in the future. The future is here but Richard has gone; he moved south ten years ago.

Populus is derived from the Latin for 'people', giving the genus the meaning 'tree of the people', but *Populus* can also mean 'crowd' and poplars often grow in congested colonies, throwing off suckers which further add to the population and crowding. *Trichocarpa* means 'hairy fruits': a trichomaniac is a hair fetishist and probably a bit of a trichophile, whereas a trichophobe is frightened of all things hairy.

Populus trichocarpa is a lovely tree and I can understand how Richard found it evocative of his earlier times. It is columnar with a grey, narrowly-fissured bark, has heart-shaped, pointed leaves from 8cm to 20cm long with the occasional 30cm long leaf making the odd appearance. The leaves are a glossy green on top, much paler and matt below, turning a lovely yellow before falling in autumn.

Reddy-brown catkins, around 10cm long, are produced in spring, indicative of a male tree; female catkins are green and produced on separate, female trees: dioecious describes plants which have male and female flowers on separate plants; monoecious describes plants which have separate male and female flowers on the same plant; and plants that have combined male and female structures in the same flower are variously labelled hermaphroditic, bisexual, androgynous and also synoecious (see June 10th).

Populus trichocarpa was the first tree to have its genome fully sequenced, at the U.S. Department of Energy Joint Genome Institute, located in Walnut Creek, California. It was discovered that there can be as much genetic difference between the leaves, roots and branches of the same tree as between unrelated trees of the same species. Does this suggest that, in some species, evolutionary change can occur within an individual organism, not only within populations?

November 24th

The Pink Fir Apple potatoes can survive pretty well in the ground so I tend to leave them there, digging them up as I need them, but with all the rain we've had, assorted rots and moulds become more likely. I dug up the rest of these potatoes today because yesterday I discovered small, black spots on potatoes from certain areas of the plot. Most of the potatoes had black growths which looked like dirt which wouldn't wash off. Some of the spots were pinhead size and others were splodges up to 5mm across.

This disease is called black scurf, easily picked off with your finger nail or scrubbed off with a vegetable brush; it doesn't do any harm to the potato tubers but it is unsightly. It's due to the fungus *Rhizoctonia solani,* which causes a wide range of plant diseases affecting things as diverse as cereals, sugar beet, cucumber and rice. Potatoes infected with black scurf should not be used for next year's seed because, even though this year's potatoes are largely unharmed by the scurf, stem canker is caused by the same fungus and pathological symptoms appear on developing shoots, resulting in damage to stems during subsequent growth.

Rhizoctonia is from Ancient Greek, 'rhizo' means 'root' and 'tonos' means 'murder'. *Solanum* is Latin for 'nightshade' and is the name of the genus to which the potatoes belong, the same genus as tomatoes, woody nightshade and deadly nightshade. When your granddad told you not to eat any green potatoes because they were poisonous, he was correct.

Scurf derives from 'scurfy', a variant of 'scurvy', from the Old Norse, 'skurfa', meaning 'crust'. Latin for 'scurvy', the sailors' disease due to a deficiency of vitamin C, is 'scorbutus'. The chemical name for vitamin C is ascorbic acid, as 'a-scorbic' means 'without scurvy'. However, I don't think feeding potatoes vitamin C will help them avoid black scurf.

November 26th

Attempts are being made to put the garden to bed for the winter. The front grass has hopefully had its last cut for the year, with mower blades raised high so that what passes for lawn is as healthy as it can be during its season of rest. The last cut should really have been a month ago but the grass has kept growing due to the mild weather, so, if it needs cut, the grass gets cut.

The front grass has no interesting fungus growing within it. It is a monoculture, the most unnatural thing in nature, Moss killer and fertilisers have been used here so little grows except the grass. These chemicals are not used on the back grass so it is much more diverse and cosmopolitan in its botany.

The last of the fallen leaves were raked up out back and the rake got all tangled up in periwinkle growing at the edge of the grass. The periwinkle was making a bid to expand its territory by spreading its liana-like stems beyond its prescribed boundary. Not only did the rake get tangled up, but my left foot got caught in the treacherous tendrils and I fell all my length into the freshly turned soil from where the Pink Fir Apples, scurf and all, had been removed two days earlier.

As I sat in the muck, I mused on the periwinkle's name, from the Latin 'per' for 'thoroughly', and 'winkle' from 'vincire', 'to bind'. This Latin root gives us the periwinkle's genus, *Vinca*. The *Vinca* that caught me was *Vinca major*, which has tiny hairs round the edges of its leaves, as opposed to *Vinca minor,* which has no hairs on the edges of its narrower leaves. I sat there with dampness insinuating upon my nether parts, consoling myself that the only thing that was injured was my dignity.

Periwinkles are considered as invasive plants in some parts of the world where they have been introduced, Australia, New Zealand, Canada, and the United States. This is no coincidence as Europeans who emigrated to these countries in centuries past took botanic mementoes to remind them of gardens at home, and some of these introductions liked their new home and flourished. *Vinca minor* was first introduced to the United States as an ornamental plant in the 1700s.

These *Vincas* contains indole alkaloids, including vincamine, which is used by the pharmaceutical industry as a precursor to vinpocetine, marketed as a nootropic agent. Nootropic agents are also called smart drugs, or cognitive enhancers. These pharmaceutical company cash cows supposedly improve memory, creativity and motivation. In a more traditional, medical context, vincamine and its derivatives are used to treat age-related and degenerative disorders. I shall look upon the periwinkles more fondly.

November 28th

Lynn and I were driving through Bilston again, from Penicuik to Edinburgh, and the day was fairly windy. We stopped at the Pentland Garden Centre which has a cute cafe that's worth a visit even if you don't want to buy any garden stuff. The southwest wind had the garden centre's three flags flying, rippling in the breeze, and herein resides some beautiful, yet normally invisible, science. There are some phenomena that you might see, but the causes of which can remain a mystery.

This mystery of why flags ripple in the wind can be considered by asking the question why flags don't fly straight out, absolutely flat from the flagpole when blown by the wind. This question and the explanation contain beauty, the beauty of fluid dynamics.

When wind or water flows round an object, it creates eddies, little whirlpools, which you can see in a stream when it flows by a stone protruding from the surface of the water. These little whirlpools, vortices, form at either side of the obstruction and continually detach from alternate sides of the blockage to move off downstream in a process called vortex-shedding. As each vortex develops, it creates a low pressure region into which the blocking object tries to move. You can't see anything happening to a rock jutting out from the surface of the water, but you can see the effect when the blockage to fluid flow (a flagpole) has an attachment, like the flags at Pentland Garden Centre.

It's worth making clear that in a scientific context, gases and liquids are fluids: fluids are substances which flow. The colloquial use of the word 'fluid' to mean a liquid in situations such as medicine is fine, as when the doctor tells you to drink plenty of fluids, but in fluid dynamics, fluids are gases and liquids.

When the wind hits a flagpole, it moves round one side creating a vortex and the associated low pressure region. This air-whirlpool moves off along the flag, sucking in that part of the flag which we see as a ripple as the invisible vortex moves along the flag. The next vortex forms on the other side of the flagpole and moves along the opposite side of the flag, producing another ripple.

Vortex formation usually occurs at a rate where we find it difficult to distinguish individual ripples so we just see a flag waving in the wind. What you can often see, and hear, especially on a windy night, is the battering of a halyard, the rope used to hoist the flag, as it is buffeted by the vortices swirling round the flagpole. If you are walking past a marina on a windy day, notice the ropes on the masts and forestays of yachts, hear them sing, and watch them dance and batter a beat against their supports, in time to the vortex-shedding.

Sometimes, given the right conditions, you can see tall cylindrical shapes react to the alternating low pressure regions caused by vortex-shedding by moving from side to side in a slow motion vibration at right angles to the wind direction. An internet search, 'M62 vortex shedding', will lead you to a 28second video-clip which has to be seen to be believed. If the science wasn't sound, you would think that this was a clip from an X-Men film, with Magneto at the height of his powers, telekinetically controlling the metal lampposts.

This type of vortex-induced vibration can have serious repercussions in engineering ventures such as bridges, chimney stacks and power transmission lines, but wind isn't the only cause. The eddies which you see in rivers and streams can be much more powerful in marine environments, affecting offshore rigs, mooring cables and the pipelines which carry oil and gas. Vortex-induced vibration is a major source of fatigue damage to these and any other structures which are in a stationary situation affected by marine currents.

You can feel the effects of vortex-shedding in water for yourself. Much of my pre-teen time was spent exploring the banks of the Ettrick and Yarrow rivers, and occasionally the riverbeds, sometimes deliberately and often accidentally. One of these trips left me bemused and confused. I was around ten years old and I knew that there had to be a scientific explanation for what I experienced, but that secret was never unveiled, not until I discovered the phenomenon of vortex-shedding many years later.

Lying on a grass bank, overhanging a four-foot-deep pool, I was irritating a ten-inch brown trout with a long stick held deep in the water. The trout would move away from the stick and I would the move the stick after it. At certain speeds, the stick would vibrate at right angles to its movement, and no matter how much I tried to stop the lateral vibration, I couldn't prevent the stick shaking. How could this be?

Twenty years after, in Edinburgh's Royal Commonwealth Pool, I was attempting to improve my technique at swimming the crawl, which, for non-swimmers, involves moving your arm through the water beneath your body. I was experimenting with different arm speeds and angles when suddenly there it was again, the same phenomenon from twenty years previously; my arm was oscillating at right angles to its movement through the water.

Another twenty years on, I was in my early fifties, teaching a topic to fourteen-year-olds on resonant frequency and the answer finally appeared. I was researching the failure of the Tacoma Narrows Bridge in 1940. The bridge was nick-named Galloping Gertie due to its propensity to oscillate in the wind. The catastrophe was caused by vertical movement of the bridge deck during severe wind conditions and, during my research, I serendipitously came across vortex-shedding as one of the proposed causes of the disaster. The fact was that it wasn't vortex-shedding which caused the bridge to collapse but something else called aeroelastic flutter, another phenomenon, but irrelevant to this story.

Realisation hit. Memories of swimming twenty years previously and of teasing a trout twenty years before were explained by vortex-shedding.

Later that same day, I was sitting in the garden, listening to sounds made by the wind, the wind in the trees and..... and the whine of telephone wires singing, another example of vortex-shedding, causing the wires above to resonate at an audible frequency.

I never knew how an Aeolian harp, sometimes called a wind harp, worked and now I did. An Aeolian harp, on a windy day, seems to play by magic with no musician in sight. But the wind is the invisible performer, caressing the strings with its delicate touch. Aeolus, the

Greek god of the wind, would smile, knowing that a human appreciates his music, not just its beauty, but the complexity of its creation and composition.

Next time you have a bath, take a pen or pencil with you. Open your legs as wide as you can and allow the water to become completely calm. Hold the pen or pencil by the pointy end with most of it vertical in the water. Move it slowly away from you. If there is a light above the bath, you should see circular shadows rotate on the bottom of the bath; these are caused by almost invisible vortices in the water as they are shed from the pencil. Move the pencil faster, at different speeds, until you feel a vibration at right angles to the pencil's movement and experience the vortex-shedding.

November 30th

The importance of colour and brightness in the garden at this time of year cannot be overstated. The Stinking iris, Gladwin iris, gladdon or roast-beef plant, are all common names, some not so common, for *Iris foetidissima*. The *Iris* genus gets its appellation from the Greek goddess of that name who was the personification of the rainbow. It alludes to the rich variety of colour displayed by the genus across species and, sometimes, within a single flower. *Foetidissima* means 'most smelly', describing the leaves when crushed, from the Latin, 'fetere', 'to stink', which gives us 'fetid', or 'foetid', however you wish to spell it.

The common name, 'roast-beef plant', hints of what the crushed foliage smells. For me, the odour is that of uncooked meat, but for others of different olfactory genetics, the smell is rotten beef. The gladdon or Gladwin names come from the Latin for 'sword', which is 'gladius', describing the sword-like shape of the leaves. This is also the root (no pun intended) for the *Gladiolus* genus, also having sword-shaped foliage, and for gladiators, swordsmen of the Roman arena.

The flowers of this plant initially look insignificant. They do not announce themselves with the glamour and ostentation of most of the genus. They are literally the wallflowers of *Iris,* in that they grow reasonably well in dry areas in heavy shade close to walls. The flowers are small and can be difficult to spot. They are a mix of dull blues and buff yellows, which do not attract a hasty gardener, but close observation is rewarded with a view of fine veining, subtle shaping and a great variety of understated, delicate colours.

The fertilised flowers develop into seedpods 5-8cm long and 3cm wide. These three-sided capsules open around this time of year to reveal what makes *Iris foetidissima* a valuable addition to any dingy corner of a dull garden; bright, orange-red seeds which persist in their pods through the winter, which catch your attention and bring brightness and colour to life through dark December's grey days.

I have seen a male blackbird eat these seeds on only two occasions so I would suspect that the seeds of *Iris foetidissima* are not their first choice of winter's brightly coloured berries. Some commentators suggest that birds avoid these seeds but I would beg to differ. My drink of choice in social situations is cask-conditioned beer, but if little else is on offer, I'll consume whatever is available. I see no reason why birds should be different. An inexperienced bird, like an inexperienced drinker, will try something until they find that it disagrees with them, or is not to their palette, and then they will move on and try something different. *Iris foetidissima* seeds may not be popular in avian circles, but if little else is on offer, they must suffice.

Circumstantial evidence of birds eating the seeds of *Iris foetidissima* is inferred from where these seeds germinate and seedlings grow. These places are the same spots where you find young plants of flowering current, cotoneaster, bramble, holly and ivy growing, such as behind my siesta-seat. This is where assorted, seed-eating birds sit in shrubs and deposit their droppings, containing undigested seeds, along with a good glob of nitrogenous fertiliser. It's not only behind the siesta-seat where these plants are to be found but in many of the shady and protected bushy areas where berry-eating birds perch. *Iris foetidissima* is found in most of these locations round my garden.

In British Birds magazine (April, 1954), the Rev. P. H. T. Hartley of the Edward Grey Institute of Ornithology, Oxford, published an article entitled, *'Wild Fruits in the Diet of British Thrushes: A Study in the Ecology of Closely Allied Species'*. Observations were recorded of which wild fruits were eaten by five species of thrush, of the genus *Turdus*. As for the popularity of the seeds of *Iris foetidissima*, Rev. Hartley writes,

> 'The Blackbird also shows a catholic choice of fruit foods (21 different fruits appearing in 745 records, as compared with only 7 fruits in 531 records in the Song Thrush)'.

The blackbird was recorded consuming 'Gladdon' on two occasions. There were no records of 'Gladdon' being eaten by any of the other four *Turdus*, Song Thrush, Mistle Thrush, Fieldfare or Redwing. So yes, blackbirds will consume the seeds of *Iris Foetidissima*, but are unlikely to do so if anything else is on offer. I'm a bit like that about certain keg beers.

December

'God gave us our memories so that we might have roses in December.'

J. M. Barrie (1860-1937)

'Before the end of December, generally, they experience their first thawing. Those which a month ago were sour, crabbed, and quite unpalatable to the civilized taste, such at least as were frozen while sound, let a warmer sun come to thaw them, for they are extremely sensitive to its rays, are found to be filled with a rich, sweet cider, better than any bottled cider that I know of, and with which I am better acquainted than with wine. All apples are good in this state, and your jaws are the cider-press.'

Henry David Thoreau (1817-1862)

'I heard a bird sing
In the dark of December
A magical thing
And sweet to remember.

'We are nearer to Spring
Than we were in September,'
I heard a bird sing
In the dark of December.'

Oliver Herford (1863-1935)

December 1st

This is the first day of official meteorological winter. It started a bit chilly but the temperature rose slightly under a *Stratus* sky. The cloud cloaked the day, and the city, with a blanket of damp, melancholic despond. Ne'er a glimpse of blue, nor a glint of the sun was seen. It was as if the weather knew that winter was upon us, and greyness was its gift.

This, for me, is the start of the SAD time of year. SAD is the acronym for Seasonal Affective Disorder. Sufferers of SAD are on a spectrum of depression from grumpiness and difficulty getting up in the morning through to depressive episodes which can be severe. It is related to the diminishment of natural light as winter approaches and the concomitant decrease in serotonin, a neurotransmitter which contributes to feelings of well-being and happiness.

There are theories that this is one of the causes of heavier alcohol intake, depression and suicide rate in populations as you move further north: the higher latitudes having longer winters with shorter days. Vitamin D is linked to serotonin levels, and its deficiency is also connected to feeling down with the winter blues. Vitamin D is synthesised in the skin, but requires sunlight's ultraviolet B rays (UVB) which is distinctly lacking in northern latitudes during winter. So what can be done to limit SAD depression?

As much time as you can manage should be spent in the open air, preferably doing something physical, during the light hours. Gardening and walking are very acceptable forms of exercise, and if you work in an office, getting out at lunchtime will benefit your physical as well as your mental health.

Waking up in the morning for work was always a problem for me so I invested in a dawn-simulating alarm clock. It was set to come on, dimly, about half an hour before getting-up time and it gradually increased in brightness until the radio-alarm went off, maintaining maximum light for another twenty minutes. My clock had a bulb, the light spectrum of which was very close to that of sunlight, and I found it very helpful. At all times of the day, whenever I was reading, I would try to ensure as great an illumination as I could manage, not only to benefit my reading, but to combat my SAD: my carbon footprint played second fiddle to my mood during the darker months.

There are various opinions as to the percentage of the Scottish adult population who are deficient in Vitamin D, some estimates greater than 50%, and this number rises with age. Vitamin D is sometimes referred to as the 'sunshine vitamin' so you should consider your diet, and if it's lacking in Vitamin D, take a supplement.

Be bald with pride. During autumn, go hatless to catch the year's last rays of UVB because Vitamin D is not quick to disappear from your system as it is stored in fat. Do not lament your bald heads: they confer evolutionary advantage, protecting you from all sorts of diseases resulting from low levels of this vitamin. Look upon bald heads as personal solar panels for the photosynthesis of vitamin D, helping ameliorate Scotland's poor cardiovascular disease, cancer statistics and SAD.

For a trait such as baldness to remain in the population, there is no necessity for it to give a positive evolutionary advantage. Such a trait will stay, so long as it doesn't confer an evolutionary disadvantage which causes carriers to be less successful than others in the gene pool. As our prehistoric ancestors moved north, not only did they lose their skin pigmentation to compensate for diminishing UVB levels with higher latitude, baldness would become an evolutionary advantage due to the greater capacity to synthesise vitamin D in the skin of the bald pate.

And more: high testosterone levels cause baldness; bald heads, on sunny days, synthesise vitamin D; and, higher levels of vitamin D are associated with higher levels of testosterone. Is this some kind of selfish-gene cycle?

I have come to like grey days, when the leaden sky is featureless, uniform in colour and texture from horizon to horizon, and when shadows are things of the past, and of the future, but not of today. These are SAD days, but activity is an antidote to SAD. I wandered the garden, tidying things that had needed tidying for weeks. Having more time allows me to notice more tasks that have been avoided, and procrastination is not a problem, but a pleasant indulgence.

I have always enjoyed the satisfaction of multi-shirking, that skill of avoiding numerous tasks simultaneously. Multi-shirking is the antithesis of multi-tasking, an activity perceived by the deluded to be noble and virtuous, but invariably leads to slapdash results and ill-considered ideas. Why synchronously do several things in a mediocre manner when you can do them so much better sequentially, or perhaps not do them at all?

The garden is tidier and my mood is mellow. Buds on trees have impending promise; tête-a-tête miniature daffodil bulbs are poking their heads through the compost in their pots, as are the garlic bulbs; blue tits, coal tits and great tits are combing the trees for insects and spiders; the grass has not yet completely succumbed to the moss; and three months after my knee replacement, I am suddenly struck by an acute awareness that there is no ache in any part of the tissues surrounding the joint, despite neglecting to take this morning's pain-killers. Grey skies are looking bright.

December 4th

Six Wood Pigeons, *Columba palumbus,* were grazing on the back lawn. The mild weather must have allowed a little fresh grass growth of which the pigeons were making the most. The Wood Pigeon is a big lump of a bird, in fact, the biggest European species of *Columba,* which is the Latin for 'pigeon'; and *palumbus* is the Latin for, specifically, the Wood Pigeon. It could be considered a dull bird because its predominant colour is grey, but that is to understate its greyness.

Its head, back, wings and rump are certainly grey, but of different shades, which change with the ambient light. Add to this, its white collar and iridescent (more about this later) green neck, its pink and orange bill, pink legs and feet, its pinkish breast fading to pale grey below and its glorious yellow eyes, the bird is a delight. Granted, on a dull day, the bird is not much to look at, but when the sun comes out, the bird can shine, literally, because the pink, upper-breast feathers are also iridescent.

The Wood Pigeon's various greys bear a strong similarity to the corrosion products of the lead that lines the junction between the roof of the kitchen and the rest of the house. Metallic lead is a bright, silvery metal which tarnishes on contact with moist air, forming a complex patina. This patina changes over time to take on the traditional 'weathered-lead' appearance that is so admired on old church roofs. So admired, that it is sometimes stolen, to be sold on as scrap, which can command a good price from dealers who don't ask too many questions.

The formation of the patina is caused by a chemical reaction called oxidation, where the metal surface combines with oxygen to form a variety of compounds, the nature of which depends on what pollutants are present in the air. These chemicals produce a hard, non-porous film which adheres to the metallic lead underneath, preventing further reaction between the metal and the atmosphere. When patination starts, it can produce an interesting optical effect called constructive interference, producing rainbow-like colours, akin to oil on water and related to the phenomenon exhibited by the pigeons' green neck feathers.

If you recall the titanium jewellery which was popular some decades ago, you may remember that it exhibited a range of colours. These colours were not due to any dye but to an oxide layer, which produces different colours depending on its thickness. The colours, which are simply different wavelengths of light, arise from light reflected from the top surface of the oxide layer combining with light reflected from the metal surface below, and are another example of iridescence.

As the patina on the lead thickens, it takes on the more familiar greys due to the presence of lead oxides, lead carbonate, lead sulphite and lead sulphate, which are insoluble and will protect the underlying lead from the meteorological elements, but sadly not from criminal elements.

The Romans used lead for their extensive plumbing systems and 'plumbing' is derived from 'plumbum', the Latin word for lead. This gives us 'plumber', originally 'lead worker', 'plumb-line', to which is fastened a lump of lead so the line hangs straight, and Pb, the symbol for lead in the Periodic Table of the Elements. This table was devised by Dmitri Mendeleev in 1869 using the 63 elements that were known at the time. There are now 118 chemical elements, 24 of which are synthetic, created by scientists.

The greys of weathered lead and the greys of *Columba palumbus* are so similar, can it be coincidence that *'palumbus'* and its accusative, 'palumbum', are so similar to 'plumbum'? Was the lead-coloured pigeon used to name lead metal, or was the metal's name used to dub the pigeon? Did an 'a' appear in 'plumbum' or disappear from 'palumbum'? Is this a pigeon and egg thing analogous the chicken and egg trope; so which came first, or is this just a coincidental, etymological omelette?

Etymology is like archaeology or palaeontology. You need stratification, a layering, a context in which you know what comes before and what comes after. This removes ambiguity. A tangible structure allows relative comparison and this is less difficult with artefacts and fossils as they constitute material evidence and their relative ages can be inferred within a time frame. With various dating techniques, the age of one artefact or fossil can be calculated which lends integrity to estimates of ages of artefacts and fossils discovered above and below the dated item.

Words do not command such specificity because the nearest you get to tangibility is the written word. It is no wonder that we can trace current language to Ancient Greek and Latin because paths, no matter how hazily indistinct, have been left on papyrus, parchment and stone, allowing us to track back and find trails and origins.

Not so with cultures which had an oral tradition. Words change with time and distance: there is no written record; the layers are confused so the etymological equivalents of the archaeological laws of superposition and stratigraphic succession are redundant; so inspired guesswork needs to be the order of the day.

December 5th

Storm Desmond brought gale force winds and a plume of moist air, known as an atmospheric river, a narrow band of moisture-laden air a few thousand miles long and a few hundred miles wide. Such air masses can carry as much water as a major world river such as the Nile. Desmond dumped its deluge on Ireland, the north of England and southern Scotland; Edinburgh got the tail end of the rain and suffered strong winds.

Last night, I was coming home from the pub through the Meadows (see October 21st), one of the capital's tree-lined parks. My usual Friday night haunt is Cloisters Bar in Brougham Street, near Toll Cross. I meet with retired teacher pals, Jim, Derrick and Ed, and assorted, occasional extras. Cloisters was formerly All Saints Parsonage House, home to the clergy of what is now Saint Michael and All Saints' Church. It still maintains an atmosphere of sanctity in that it has no TV screens, the blight of many formerly fine bars; no music, other than the clink of glasses and the hum of contented drinkers; and no gambling machines, as all money which comes out of patrons' pockets goes into the till behind the bar.

School pupils like to imagine that their teachers may have a life outside of school and pupils may enquire about what teachers get up to at the weekend. Jim, Derrick and I taught at the same school for a long time, often teaching the children of parents whom we once taught. Pupils knew we met each other on a Friday night, and they would ask what we got up to. We more or less told the truth by informing them that we went to a philosophy club at a church, where we discussed politics, the social problems of the day and how to put them right. Some kids would nod acceptingly, look at us strangely then head off along the school corridor. The street-wise would look at us suspiciously, 'Aye, right' style, then accuse us of going to the pub. How trusting and untrusting some children can be.

On the way home from Cloisters, I stood amongst the Meadows' leafless trees and closed my eyes. The sounds of wind in trees are so like the sounds of water. As the type and density of the trees, and the strength of the wind varies, you can be transported to different aquatic environments; sometimes the sea, by a beach or on the open ocean, sometimes a small stream or a huge river. Last night in Desmond's gales, I was returned to Gullfoss, visited by Lynn and me in 1983.

Gullfoss is an Icelandic waterfall which is fed from the Lángjökull glacier, Iceland's second largest. The waters, which average a flow of 140 cubic metres per second, pour down a wide, curved, ten metre, three-step stair, before plunging over an eleven metre drop followed by a second drop of twenty two metres. Thirty three years later, I can still feel the noise and hear the strength and power; to stand by Gullfoss was to be immersed in the beauty and magnificence of nature.

With eyes closed beneath the trees in the Meadows, I was back there in Iceland, the clout and roar of the wind echoing the power and roar of the Gullfoss, so many years ago, but feeling as if yesterday.

How Lynn and I agreed to go to Iceland was down to a combination of my smart-arsery and hubris. I've never been particularly keen on travelling and after ten years of holidaying in Scotland, Lynn was insistent that we go on a holiday abroad. I thought that I could avert this possibility by pompously announcing that the only foreign country I was willing to visit was Iceland and, because it was so expensive, I would only consider camping. The last thing which I expected Lynn to say was that Iceland was always a place which had captured her imagination and which she would love to visit. Hubris jumped up and bit my smart arse.

Camping in Iceland in July is like camping in Scotland in April, four seasons in one day: but both brilliant and memorable, nevertheless.

December 6th

Storm Desmond has come and gone, following its siblings, storms Abigail, Barney and Clodagh, out into the North Sea, and probably beyond. A visit from Desmond was like a visit from a rumbustious relative; a clear-up is required after they have departed. I wandered the garden picking up branches and twigs, pleased to find that, just as the boisterous relative may leave a thank-you present to be discovered after they have left, Storm Desmond's mild air and moisture had coaxed more mushrooms to make an appearance.

Another waxcap, a *Hygrocybe,* had poked some yellow-orange caps through the grass. They could be the same as had gone before, or they could be *Hygrocybe quieta,* the Oily Waxcap, sometimes called the Tranquil Waxcap, 'Tranquil' and *quieta* alluding to its inconspicuousness.

I also spotted three more mushrooms, growing close together, of a species which I hadn't seen before. They belonged to the genus *Stropharia,* and were either, *Stropharia caerulea,* the Blue

Roundhead, or *Stropharia aeruginosa,* the Verdigris Roundhead. The caps were a greeny-grey or verdigris colour on top with a more bluish border towards the edge. The species names, *aeruginosa,* means 'bluish-green', and *caerulea,* means 'blue'. I was quite chuffed to think that I could identify the genus of this mushroom with a high probability of being *Stropharia,* and the species likely to be *caerulea* or *aeruginosa.*

These *Stropharia* mushrooms were pretty to look at and, as I found out over the next week, their colours change with time, and also with humidity, so goodness knows whether the species was *caerulea* or *aeruginosa.* Who'd be a taxonomist?

December 7th

Waking up to the sound of chain saws and an industrial wood-grinder is not a way that I would advocate to start a day. A neighbour across the road was having two large lime trees removed from his garden. The common lime tree, *Tilia vulgaris,* can grow up to a hundred and fifty feet tall with an eight-foot diameter trunk, not a tree for an urban garden. One of the trees being removed was damaging the boundary wall, causing the mortar between the sandstone blocks to fall out. The two trees were to the south-west of my house so they blocked the afternoon sun and the view to the Royal Observatory on Blackford Hill and the Pentland Hills beyond: I was not sorry to see them go.

The lime tree, or linden, is a majestic, wildlife-friendly tree, but it needs to be grown in an ample area to be appreciated, so the question must be asked why anyone would plant such vigorous trees in obviously limited space? The answer to (and blame for) why people plant such large trees in an inappropriate place does not lie with the current occupants of houses in the Grange and in other quarters of Edinburgh where Lime trees are frequently to be found pushing against and damaging walls. It lies with our predecessors from between one hundred and two hundred years ago.

Many of the nineteenth century houses in the Grange are surrounded by handsome stone walls. Lime trees were planted behind walls to form a row at a distance apart which, after a few years, allowed the immature crowns to grow together to form an impressive raised hedge. Some of these rows of lime trees may even have been pleached, where the young branches of a tree were interwoven with those of the adjacent trees. If you have seen avenues of pleached trees in formal gardens then you will appreciate that the perception of control over nature made these practices popular, particularly in the eighteenth century when the likes of landscape gardener Capability Brown were horticultural icons.

The problem was that the preservation of lime avenues, whether pleached or not, was a high maintenance task. The very reason that lime trees grow fast meant that your raised hedge formed within a few years, but also that the same hedge became a problem very quickly if the trees were not controlled. This is analogous to the Leyland cypress hedge problems of today; both lime and Leylandii can grow three feet a year in favourable conditions.

If you look closely at the structure of mature, urban lime trees, you will see that about a third of the way up, where the main trunk divides into several lesser trunks there is evidence of repeated cutting back. This shows that these trees have been pollarded. Pollarding is a system in which the upper branches of a tree are removed, promoting a dense head of foliage and branches, which in the case of lime trees, results in them looking like giant mushrooms.

The rural practice of pollarding, like coppicing, was to encourage trees to produce new growth to supply wood for a variety purposes, but mostly for fuel. In coppicing, the cutting occurs at around three feet above ground level, whereas with pollarding, the cutting is at a height above that which browsing animals could feed, thus protecting the fresh, young shoots.

Once lime trees got beyond a certain height, even if they had been previously pollarded, new house owners would be disinclined to spend a lot of money to bring them back under control. We have today's result that an awful lot more money is required to rectify a potentially damaging situation, because lime trees will push over walls. I can understand why, over the last fifty years or so, limes have been left to their own devices. Who is going to pay for regular pollarding? A stitch in time saving nine is all very well, but not when the result is a row of big sticks with pompoms on top. What we have is a fashion that has literally outgrown its popularity.

Tilia vulgaris or, more correctly these days, *Tilia × europaea*, is a naturally occurring hybrid between *Tilia cordata*, the small-leaved lime and *Tilia platyphyllos,* the large-leaved lime. The species names describe leaf shape; *cordata* means 'heart-shaped' and *platyphyllos* means 'broad leaf', like a plate.

There is a booklet called *'Trees in the Grange'*, produced for The Grange Association and available to read on their website (gaedin.co.uk). In it, Alistair Scott wrote that in the 1972 survey of trees in the Grange, the Edinburgh area where I live, 12% of the tree stock was of the genus, *Tilia*.

'Trees in the Grange' is wonderfully informative about all things arboreal relative to suburban gardens: trees we can do without; the five steps to choosing a new tree; lists of possibilities; the four golden rules of management and pruning practicalities; and so much more. Alistair includes in the first golden rule of management and pruning, that you do nothing until you have imagined, with as much precision as possible, what might be done to a tree. You should live with that imagined future for a while, and to couple this with a deckchair on a warm day and a glass of something soothing while contemplating the object of your attention.

The leaves of *Tilea* are edible, especially the young ones which can be added to salads, but you might be averse to their muciligenous nature, slimy when chewed; think mucous. The fibrous inner bark, known as 'bass' or 'bast', has been used since prehistory to make rope, string, fabric and nets. The wood is soft and finely textured, making it is easy to work and it is often used in turnery, carving and furniture-making. Again in prehistoric times, it was used to construct dug-out canoes. The flowers provide nectar and pollen for insects, particularly bees, and they can be dried and used to make herbal teas and tinctures, traditionally to treat colds, coughs, fever and infections. Active ingredients, besides mucilage, include tannin astringents and flavanoid antioxidants.

Over millennia, *Tilia* has been a great benefit to humankind, and only recently, in the last fifty years, has it become a nuisance. This is not through any fault of *Tilia*, but through injudicious planting, where trees outgrow their site. Lime trees are very attractive to aphids and one consequence of planting lime trees alongside roads is that the aphids produce large amounts of a sugary liquid called honeydew, which drops on to cars parked underneath. This modern-day irritation could be blamed on street planners from a hundred years ago being unable to predict the advent of roadside-parking which would be required by citizenry once the planners were dead and gone. On the other hand, the modern-day, irritated citizen could learn to identify *Tilia* and park their car somewhere else, but I suspect that the learning, the identifying and the re-parking would be too much effort for some.

Despite lime trees being very common in Scotland, especially in cities, it may come as a surprise to discover that no *Tilia* is native to this country. Donald Pigott, the doyen of all things *Tilia*, describes his reasons for holding this opinion in *'A Handbook of Scotland's Trees, the essential guide for enthusiasts, gardeners and woodland lovers to species cultivation, habits, uses and lore'*, edited by Fi Martynoga for Reforesting Scotland.

In the chapter, 'Lime, *Tilia spp'* (*sp* means species and *spp* is the plural), Donald Pigott explains how *Tilia* pollen is identified but, somewhat unusually, that the pollen from different *Tilia* species can be easily distinguished. If *Tilia* pollen is found in samples of peat, or any other deposit, then lime trees were present when that deposit was laid down. Pollen analyses for northern England and southern Scotland show no evidence for native lime trees north of the border; the northern limit for indigenous lime trees was to the south of the border.

All told, I was sad to see my neighbour's two lime trees get the chop (and the grind), but the south-west perspective now allows me a panoramic view to the Royal Observatory and the Pentland Hills in the distance.

December 10th

'Plausible deniability', or the idea which these two words represent has probably been around since language evolved, but the expression 'plausibly deniable' came to the fore in US politics around 1974. A US Senate committee found that the CIA had plotted to assassinate certain foreign leaders, but the President was kept out of the loop, even though he agreed with the wider concept, so he could ' plausibly deny' any knowledge of it.

If you know someone who actively avoids information, 'Don't tell me. I don't want to know', who understands that the lack of this knowledge will be to their benefit as it cannot come back to haunt them, then that person is attempting to build a defence of plausible deniability in the event of future accusations.

At the USLegal website (definitions.uslegal.com) in 'Plausable (sic) Deniability Law and Legal Definition', the definition of 'Plausible deniability' goes,

'Plausable (sic) deniability refers to circumstances where a denial of responsibility or knowledge of wrongdoing cannot be proved as true or untrue due to a lack of evidence proving the allegation. This term is often used in reference to situations where high ranking officials deny responsibility for or knowledge of wrongdoing by lower ranking officials. In those situations officials can 'plausibly deny' an allegation even though it may be true'.

Previously, it was two rogue programmers. Today, the press reported that Volkswagen has suspended nine managers suspected of involvement in the manipulation of diesel emissions tests using cheat-devices. How many more? What's Volkswagen-speak for 'plausible deniability'?

If the board at Volkswagen think that nine suspended managers will put the scandal to rest then their thoughts are undeniably implausible.

December 11th

Jealousy is not part of my nature but when I go out for a newspaper, I walk past Judith and Alistair's garden which sports a hydrangea, *Hydrangea macrophylla,* of which I am more than a little envious. The flowers have normally lost their allure and colour by now, but once again, the clement weather has helped the object of my mild envy retain its beautiful deep blue, unlike the grotty and pallid pink of my *Hydrangea macrophylla.*

The colour of a hydrangea can be affected by changing the acidity, or pH, of the soil in which it grows. Lowering the pH by adding acidic matter to the soil, such as ericaceous compost, designed for acid-loving plants like heather, will make the flowers blue. Adding lime, an alkaline substance, the opposite of acidic, will raise the pH and make the flowers pink.

Every couple of years, various acidic materials have been dug into the soil around my hydrangea but all to no avail. My hydrangea grows next to the wall in a position where a lot of the old lime mortar has spoiled and washed out, leaving the hard Portland cement mortar, naively used to repair pointing applied in the twentieth century, standing proud of the eroding sandstone. The name tells the tale; 'lime' mortar from the wall will neutralise acid in the soil, keeping my hydrangea pink. Judith and Alistair's hydrangea is well away from any wall and the acid-neutralising effect of its mortar.

Fun can be had with pH. Many plant chemicals will change colour depending on the pH of their environment and such chemicals are termed pH indicators. Anthocyanins are responsible for the red colour in red onions, red apples and red grapes but best of all, in red cabbage. If you boil or steam red cabbage, keep the left-over liquid. It contains the anthocyanin pigment that gives the cabbage its colour.

Impress a small child with your wizardry by pouring the purple cabbage water into three glasses you prepared earlier: one containing a little white vinegar, one with a little baking soda and one with a little water. The acidic vinegar turns the cabbage water red, the alkaline baking soda turns the cabbage water green and water should maintain the purple colour with which you started. Once you have explained what was going on, let the child test lots of kitchen chemicals with the cabbage water, under supervision of course, while wearing cycling glasses, or even sunglasses, to protect the eyes. You may want to suggest removing tinted glasses to view and appreciate the colours.

December 12th

The practice of adorning windows and gardens with lights in the lead-up to Christmas seems to get earlier every year. So long as it's not too gaudy, people can do whatever they like if it doesn't disturb the local wildlife. We are nearing that time of year when nights are longest and days, if skies are blanketed grey, hardly seem to brighten at all. There have been times recently when security lights, designed to come on in the dark when they detect intruders, have switched on in the middle of the day when innocents are going about my garden.

People have an innate desire to lessen the darkness of winter and are drawn to that light and warmth which generally accompanies their efforts to brighten their lives. It is only from the late nineteenth century that electrical lights have taken over from fire and flame, and one hundred and fifty years is but a blink of an eye in human history.

Natural selection picks those who survive to pass on their genes, and those who would have been most successful were those ancestors who could ameliorate the raw conditions of prehistoric existence by the judicious use and pleasure of fire. Archaeologists have evidenced hearths and campfires from at least a million years ago; that's 50,000 generations who have huddled round fires enjoying the heat, the dance of the flame, the crackle and hiss, the colours, and the smells of drying clothing and the cooking of food. Cooked food supplies around 30% more energy than raw food, facilitating chewing and digestion. Some believe that this was the catalyst to the development of the bigger brains of modern humans (I use the word 'modern' in the context of human evolution and that means over the last 200,000 years).

A fire gives focus to social interaction, where communication, culture and language would mutually support the development of each. Sitting round a fire feels good. Watching dancing lights is entrancing. There is positive neurological feedback in the relaxing non-activity of fire-gazing. Staring into the chaotic transmogrifications of fire is magical and meditative. Through flame, our ancestors would see the solid and substantial transformed to the ethereal and insubstantial, then carried to the skies. No wonder then that funeral pyres became part of so many cultures' religious ritual. Fire transports, from this world to a different world, a spiritual ghost world hidden from view.

Brains and bodies are in constant communication, whether a snail's, a snake's or a human's. Our body parts detect our environment giving constant update about risks and rewards, and messages are sent to our brain, our central processing unit. Through a combination of nature, experience ingrained through evolution, and experience gained through our life, the brain makes decisions on how to act, unconsciously or consciously, depending on the situation. Messages are sent to the appropriate parts of your body so the right action to promote your survival is taken. You run away fast or you get aggressive if the fight-or-flight reaction kicks in; you dip your finger into the sweet honey in a bees' nest if you calculate that the benefit outweighs the risk; or you find yourself standing on a chair screaming at a mouse or spider because your embedded nature from millions of years of evolution conflicts and prevails over your experiential knowledge. So why does sitting round a fire feel good? How can there be a positive, neurological feedback?

Christopher Lynn of the Department of Anthropology, University of Alabama, Tuscaloosa, supplies some evidence. In the journal, Evolutionary Psychology (Nov 11, 2014), he had an article published called, '*Hearth and campfire influences on arterial blood pressure: defraying the costs of the social brain through fireside relaxation*'.

He hypothesised that,

> '....calmer, more tolerant people would have benefited in the social milieu via fireside interactions relative to individuals less susceptible to relaxation response'.

His results showed that watching a campfire gave consistent decreases in blood pressure, particularly with a longer duration of fire-watching. He concluded that,

> '....findings confirm that hearth and campfires induce relaxation as part of a multisensory, absorptive, and social experience'.

Take away the campfire and go to a sports bar where at least one TV screen can be seen from every seat or stance. Different screens may show different sports, some with the sound turned off. I have found my eyes drifting, when there is a lull in the conversation, to a screen showing darts or snooker, 'sports' in which I have no particular interest, but somehow a feeling of relaxation is still induced. Could it be that the bright, moving colours on the screen replace the shifting flames in my evolutionary psyche? Maybe, it's just the drink.

In their homes, some people have a TV switched on with the sound off, perhaps for company, or perhaps the movement of colours on the screen helps them relax. Even more intriguing, you can get hours-long videos of crackling fires which should seem pretty pointless, but which, when I checked them out, I found quite engrossing and meditative. The caveman's disposition may be closer to the surface of our character than we might dare to think.

December 13th

The first really cold night arrived and left a hoar frost on the grass and pretty patterns of feathers and ferns on the roof and windscreen of the car. 'Hoar' is a funny old word having nothing to do with any other word of similar pronunciation. 'Hoar' or 'hoary' means venerable or elderly, and, as an archaic adjective, describes someone having greying or white hair.

There's more than one kind of frost. The hoar frost which makes the pretty patterns on the car and turns the grass white forms in a different way from the frost you get on your windscreen which looks like droplets of frozen rain.

With clear, winter skies, the temperature drops at night and surfaces radiate heat energy out towards the sky: the surfaces actually have a lower temperature than the air above. When a surface cools below the freezing point of water, ice crystals can form at nucleation points on that surface. Nucleation sites are tiny imperfections that allow crystals of ice to start to grow. These points can be microscopic scratches or bits of dirt that give molecules a foothold. A similar process can be observed with a fizzy drink: streams of bubbles form at nucleation sites on the sides and bottom of the glass.

Once minuscule ice crystals form, water molecules from the air attach to the ice crystals causing them to grow. The water molecules go straight from a gas to a solid, missing out the liquid phase. As the gaseous water molecules can only join to the solid ice crystals at very particular angles, beautiful shapes can appear. If the feather and fern-like shapes are examined closely, you will often see that similar patterns recur at progressively smaller scales. Such a pattern is called a fractal, a term first used by the mathematician Benoît Mandelbrot who, in 1975, used it to describe geometric patterns in nature, patterns which repeat at different magnifications. The shape of coastlines, trees, algal growth, lightning and Romanesco cauliflower all show aspects of a fractal character.

The frost that looks like frozen rain forms differently. When the sun goes down and it's not too cold, only cold enough to form dew, then that's what forms on your car roof and windscreen. Later in the night, if the cloud dissipates and the sky clears, the temperature will drop. This can result in the dew drops freezing to give you a view out of your car the following morning as if you are looking through pebbled glass, nice enough but not nearly as attractive as the fractal frost.

Either type of frozen windscreen can be very irritating if you are pushed for time on a cold morning, but a few minutes to appreciate their aesthetics from inside the car, looking out, is time well spent in my mind.

The next time you remove hoar frost's icy feathers and ferns from your windscreen, take a few moments to appreciate its fractacalities, before addressing the practicalities of destroying nature's frozen graffiti with your de-icer or scraper. Beauty is ephemeral and often goes unnoticed before it disappears or is destroyed: appreciate Jack Frost's artistry and your day, which may have started with a chill, will end up making you feel warm inside..

December 15th

Despite the frost of the last few nights, the Yellow Fumitory, or Yellow Corydalis, *Corydalis lutea,* is remarkably still flowering: it usually flowers from May to October. It grows in cracks in the wall, with lots of racemes of yellow, trumpet-like flowers which have a spur, shaped like the crest on a bird's head, from which it gets the *Corydalis* name from the Greek for 'crested lark': *lutea* means yellow. Once it colonises an old wall or cracked paving, Yellow Corydalis is hard to get rid of, not that I'd want to. It is a prolific self-seeder and can survive a very dry environment, hence it can grow in mortared walls, and it is happy in shade or sun. To refer to this plant as low-maintenance is to exaggerate how much work is required to keep it looking good; no-maintenance would be a better description. Some may consider *Corydalis lutea* a weed but I judge it a golden gift.

Corydalis lutea has been reclassified as *Pseudofumaria lutea* to form the *Pseudofumaria* genus with *Pseudofumaria alba,* the only other species in the genus, and the much paler cousin of *Pseudofumaria lutea.*

The wall on which the Yellow Corydalis grows only catches some late-day sun at the height of summer, so it brightens the north-west facing wall in a mild winter. It grows alongside the Common Snowberry, *Symphoricarpos albus,* another potentially invasive weed; but I like it for the same reasons as I like the Corydalis. It brightens a dull corner at a dull time of year, with little maintenance, other than to haul some out when it gets a bit overconfident.

The snowberry's botanical name comes from the Greek, 'symphora' for 'gathering' and 'carpos' for 'fruit'. *Symphoricarpos* describes the closely squashed-together berries that come after the small, pretty, pink flowers. The flowers may be insignificant but the white berries are conspicuous, as they need to be, to attract the birds which eat them in order that the seeds inside the berries can be dispersed.

The pheasant and grouse, which eat snowberries, are immune to the cocktail of alkaloids, and some other unpleasant, physiologically active chemicals, which the berries harbour. This mixture would cause you and me delirium, dizziness and serious vomiting if we ate a few. The vomiting is a good thing because it rids you of the nasty chemicals before they can do you any serious harm. Because of this, there are few cases of Snowberry poisoning, along with the fact that white berries look particularly unappetising. One of the Snowberry's common names, on the other side of the Atlantic Ocean, is that used by the North American First Nations peoples who called it the Corpse Berry or Ghost Berry, because the berries were supposedly eaten by the wandering dead.

December 17th

A couple of nights of frost and low, single-figure temperatures during the day have hinted that we might have made a start to winter. The average daily temperature for December in this part of the country is 6°C, but today's temperature is 13°C. Despite the well-above-average temperature, the siesta-seat is now just a seat as it is of little use for a snooze in the sun at this time of year: the sun is too low at Edinburgh's latitude of 56°north. At midday, the sun reaches an elevation of less than 12° above the horizon and just manages to peek over the neighbouring roofs.

There is some sun on the seat, for about half an hour, but this is interrupted by chimney shadows slowly traversing the bench. To stay in the sun, if it deigns to show itself, I shuffle along the seat from right to left, followed by the shadow of a chimney stack. As I reach the end of the bench, I get up and move to the right side of the chimney's shadow and, in turn, follow it until it drops of the bench. This is followed by the shadow of another chimney pushing me along the seat; and so it continues until the sun sinks below a roof ridge and I have to make a decision.

Do I go indoors, or is there enough heat in the sun to enjoy it in the north corner of the garden, the last place in the garden to lose the full sun as it drops behind the roof? If I disdain indoors and choose the north corner, I'll position myself, standing, facing south, with eyes closed, and meditate on the bright light trying to sear through my eyelids and enjoy any warmth on my face.

When I find myself internally verbalising the thoughts and conversations that buzz around my brain, I try to stop the mental dialogue and concentrate on my posture, imagining a hook in the topmost part of my head pulling me upwards, so that I am tall, straight and stretched as I can be, with my feet still flat on the ground. This exercise maintains the muscles of the back, neck and of the abdominal core. This keeps you walking tall and holds aging at bay: think of an elderly person you know with excellent posture and you'll be thinking of an elderly person who appears young for their years. A younger person with poor posture will seem to have aged prematurely.

If the buzz in my head persists, I concentrate on my breathing: inhale for a count of four, then hold the inhalation for another count of four; exhale for a count of four then hold the exhalation, again for count of four; and then repeat for as long as concentration can be maintained. If you try this, you may find that the 'holds' are difficult so hold for a count of two, or don't hold at all, and, if you feel dizzy, stop. That is, stop the exercise, don't stop the breathing; and with a little practice, tranquillity is the prize.

The sun dropped behind the roof ridge and I stopped the exercise. The corner behind me is a bit of a jungle, deliberately so. Of the wall that surrounds the garden, this part would have been easiest for an intruder to gain entrance due to a sycamore tree growing on the other side.

A bygone and brutal practice, but probably very successful, was to discourage wall-climbers and trespassers by cementing broken glass to the top of such walls. Many of the houses in the Grange were built before the advent of barbed wire, which was invented in the 1860s in the USA, as a means of preventing cattle from roaming free. It would have taken some years, or decades, for barbed wire to reach Edinburgh, so the few walls that are left in the Grange and still topped with broken glass were probably thus adorned by the original builders or owners of the properties.

Shunning broken glass and barbed wire, I've given nature a helping hand in intruder-discouragement by planting a holly tree in this northern corner of the garden. This was about twenty years ago and, ten years after, I added a rambling rose which rambles through the holly tree, along and over the wall, announcing its prickly presence to any potential prowlers.

Nature has taken over. As it's difficult to get anywhere near the corner now, whatever germinates and thrives on the ground below the holly is almost unreachable. The unreachables which add to the corner-security scheme are a large buddleia with lots of sharp, broken branches. They could take out an unwary interloper's eye, if they were stupid enough to take on the holly spines and the rose thorns. There is an extra dissuasion below, a bed of stinging nettles.

Very carefully, I stuck my head into the jungle to see if anything new was growing, if anything had died, or if anything had been left by neighbours' pets or wildlife. The only thing of note was an abundance of Jelly Ear fungus, growing on the bark of the buddleia, but never before seen in such profusion. The Jelly Ear, *Auricularia auricula-judae,* has undergone a number of changes to its common name and caused arguments, if not convulsions, amongst mycologists with regard to its scientific name.

This brown, ear-shaped fungus grows on wood, particularly the elderberry, the tree from which, Judas Iscariot, the apostle and betrayer of Jesus, hanged himself, according to history or mythology, depending on your standpoint. The species name, *auricula-judae,* is the Latin for 'ear of Judas' and there was some opinion among mycologists that *judae,* for reasons of political correctness, should be dropped to give *Auricularia auricula* as the correct scientific name for the fungus. This dispute apparently continues, but passively, as both *Auricularia auricula-judae* and *Auricularia auricula* are used by different mycological authorities.

The fungus has had many common names over time, changing from Judas's Ear, to Judas' Ear, to Jew's Ear, and now to the more generally acceptable Jelly Ear, thus avoiding any possible derogatory allusion. Some may consider the name change to 'Jelly Ear' from 'Jew's Ear' as an oversensitive regard for political correctness. But there are always racists who will see any term, from their warped viewpoint which condones discrimination, as a peg on which to hang their bigoted hat, so I go with Jelly Ear. Jelly Ear is also an excellent description of the fully hydrated fruiting-body of the fungus.

Recipes abound for this fungus and some members of the *Auricularia* genus are grown commercially for food in China. I haven't cooked Jelly Ear but I've had a chew at the uncooked item. To me, it is utterly tasteless, though a mild tingling on the tongue persisted for an hour after chewing. I didn't swallow; it is one thing to consider yourself quite brave when sampling new foods, but it is quite another to be foolhardy. The texture, however, is interesting, so I can understand why some may like finely chopped Jelly Ear in a pasta dish, or with a well-seasoned sauce. A culinary attribute is that the Jelly Ear can be stored dried and can be reconstituted by soaking before cooking; it may be that cooking brings out some flavour that the uncooked version lacks; experimental gastronomes take note.

Auricularia auricula-judae has long been used in traditional medicine and recent research has shown anti-tumour, anti-coagulant and anti-cholesterol activities. It would be unwise to assume that *Auricularia auricula-judae* is some sort of panacea as, like all medicines, there is a fine line between the dazzling, therapeutic attributes and the darker side-effects of any pharmacological star. There are reports of cases of internal bleeding in people who ate too much sweet-and-sour soup, combined with stir-fry, both containing Jelly Ear.

Painkillers like aspirin or ibuprofen have exactly the same anti-coagulant effect, but their therapeutic attributes are supported by randomised, double-blind, placebo-controlled, clinical studies. Alternative medicine is an alternative to things that have been proven to work.

December 18th

Remember 'plausible deniability' (see December 10th). Some people and some corporations have, as my mother would have said while shaking her head and looking downwards in an introspective manner, 'Nae shame.' Volkswagen, under the Skoda label, has sent us another nice letter about our car with the emissions-cheat software, described by Volkswagen as the 'diesel engines NOx emissions issue', which they are 'taking very seriously', and so they should! I don't get angry very often.

First, it was two rogue programmers, and then it was nine suspended managers. Now, it's reported that at least thirty top managers were in on the emissions-cheating devices, involving eleven million cars worldwide. Graham Ruddick, in the Guardian (December 17th, 2015), reports that the carmaker has almost halved the number of senior managers reporting to the chief executive. This is a fine money-saving exercise as Volkswagen may need these salaries to employ more lawyers, methinks.

The European Union's anti-fraud office is investigating loans totalling an estimated 9.5 billion euros (£6.9bn) which Volkswagen received from the European Investment Bank to develop cleaner engines! This is another prime case of the importance of presentation over substance because the engines certainly presented as being cleaner and greener to the emissions testers, so obviously money well spent. Hubris does have a cute way of biting even corporate butts.

The nice letter tells us that the solution to our car's ability to lie to emissions testers will only take around thirty minutes to rectify, using a software update. They also tell us that their

> '....objective is to achieve the applicable emissions targets without affecting engine output, fuel consumption and performance. However, as all model variants have to be measured first, we cannot give a final confirmation of results just yet'.

That's like me saying that my objective is to be younger, fitter and brainier but there are a number of things that will need sorted first, not the least, my age, health and intelligence.

Volkswagen/Skoda writes,

> 'We of course won't charge you for implementing the necessary measures, and we will do our utmost to minimise any inconvenience including, if required, keeping you mobile while the work is carried out.'

They are nice people. They're not going to charge me for Volkswagen/Skoda actively lying to owners and nations, while the vehicles which they sold to us spew illicit poison into our air. They must have heard about my knee operation because, like Lynn and my surgeon, they want to keep me mobile. Note the language; Volkswagen did not say that they would supply replacement cars if affected owners needed them; a fine back-out clause if they are unable to supply replacement vehicles. Perhaps they have bought in an emergency supply of bus passes and Oyster cards.

On a more positive note today, a pleasant evening was spent in Cloisters drinking some excellent beer from the Alchemy Brewery in Livingston. The ale on offer was Ritual, a fine, pale ale with an alcohol content of 4.1% which makes for easy drinking. It has flavours of light malt with a hint of biscuit plus citrus, floral overtones. Derek, a Cloister regular, was very happy as the Malt of the Moment, the discount whisky on offer at Cloisters, was from a distillery on the island of Islay. Islay is the home of some of the strongest-flavoured malt whiskies, a property which endears them to Derek, but is less appreciated by others.

Islay whiskies tend to be dry, phenolic and peaty but can be gentler, mossy rather than peaty, if distilled in the north of the island, like the Bunnahabhain on offer tonight. Jim likes the southern Islay malts with their medicinal, carbolic, smoky flavour and bite, whereas Ed's whisky predilections tend to Speyside, from where the whisky has an underlying fruitiness from maturation in sherry casks.

Where does that leave me when whisky's on the table? I get to sniff their empty glasses, which I thoroughly enjoy. I have been blessed with genes that preclude me from appreciating the taste of whisky. Its flavours, I can enjoy, but only through the sense of smell, a small mercy for which I am thankful as the richness, profusion and variety of aromas which whisky provides is an olfactory delight.

When whisky touches a tongue, taste sensors fire and send off neurological messages to the brain, to the primary gustatory cortex, the structure responsible for the perception of taste and gauging the intensity of sourness, bitterness, sweetness, salt and umami. Derek's, Jim's and Ed's genes are expressed differently from mine in how these flavours and their intensities are detected, and in how they are perceived and appreciated. There is observational evidence for this.

When Derek raises his whisky glass to his mouth, a hint of a Mona Lisa smiles plays on his lips before he sips a little of the single malt whisky. As the Bunnahabhain rolls round Derek's palette, there is a visible relaxation in his features, his eyes half close and noises, like those of a contented cat, come from deep within. His shoulders relax and drop slightly as any tension in the neck muscles is released, and languor travels from his taste buds to his tippy-toes. This is the Islay Effect, a spiritual experience.

When *any* whisky gets anywhere near my palette, my primary gustatory cortex perceives danger, probably recognising whisky for the poison it is, and unconsciously communicates with emotional centres and motor areas in my brain to make me instantaneously eject the toxin-laden liquid. My cultural and social training will hopefully continue to conquer my reflex reaction to spit the whisky from my mouth, and this self-control maintains barroom etiquette.

Your brain is continually monitoring your body's environment through your sensory system. It takes decisions, of which you may be only remotely conscious, in its role as your protector-in-chief. It is the guardian of your heritable legacy and does this to keep you whole and healthy so that your genetic gifts can be passed to future generations. The guardian of my genetic legacy allows me to savour whisky's spiritual bouquet but not its tangible taste.

December 19th

The midday sun was kissing my closed eyes under the pine tree and I was enjoying the short moments when the sun caresses the siesta-seat at this time of year so close to the solstice. There was a steady wind and the temperature was a comfortable 14°C, hard to believe. I was sitting, wide awake, despite eyes shut, listening to the trees. The arboreal soundscape is different now since the deciduous trees have shed their leaves.

The Scots pines are shy singers during the spring, summer and autumn, leaving the stage to the birch, poplar and sycamore which are louder, their branches acting as wind instruments and their foliage as soft percussion. Now these trees are naked and unable to play their music, unless the wind blows strong. The pine trees sing with sounds akin to the open sea, but more muted, a melancholic lament for the year near done.

So much for wide awake; I dozed off and woke a half hour later. How I slept, I don't know because the sun was gone, the temperature had dropped a couple of degrees, the wind had risen and the birch, poplar and sycamore had decided that they had been quiet long enough. They weren't being particularly loud, but their pitch was deep, baritone and base. The aquatic setting had moved from ocean to river, a big river. The sibilant hiss of the conifers combined with the deeper throaty sighs of the bare birch and poplar to evoke memories as a child, standing by the River Ettrick in flood. It reminded me of the night, a couple of weeks ago in the Meadows when storm Desmond visited, when I was returned to Gullfoss (see December 5th). Something was lacking though, something elusive, but I wasn't sure what.

I got out of siesta-seat and stood under the birch. The wind was now blowing a hooley and the noise took me right back, fifty-odd years to 1963, by the banks of the Ettrick.

My mother, father and eight year old me, with infant sister, Jackie, in a buggy, were out a walk by the River Ettrick: it was in spate. We walked a path called the Damside, by a manmade waterway, which I didn't know then was the mill lade which supplied energy to power the woollen mill which we had earlier walked passed. Our objective was Morris Cauld, a weir built across the Ettrick to divert the water which drove the mill. The Cauld is almost hundred metres wide and the full force of the Ettrick was flowing over it and it is some force: when the Ettrick is in flood, it is the second fastest river in Scotland, beaten only by the Spey.

The sound was deafening as the water cascaded over the slope of the Cauld, to produce a four-foot standing wave at the bottom. Two or three salmon each minute would erupt from the base of the standing wave and leap onto the cauld, their tails thrashing rapidly from side to side, propelling them up and over the weir, driven by their reproductive imperative. Their spawning grounds lay beyond, in the streams and burns which supply the waters of the Ettrick and the Yarrow, the confluence of which was about four hundred metres above the Cauld.

Eyes closed in the garden, the time machine that is memory carried me to the Cauld that day in 1963. I tarried a while until my mental Tardis returned me to today beneath the birch, but today's impression was askew; the sensation differed from that in my memory of standing by the swollen River Ettrick. The recollection held the feeling of magnificent power which turbulent water conveys and I could hear this strength in the wind and the trees, but the memory also held something more subtle, something you feel, that is neither sight nor sound, something more palpable that is not replicated by wind in trees. Standing by a rapid river in flood, you can feel its power through your feet. It is a semiconscious sensation, something aberrant, near preternatural; you know it is there but it is difficult to articulate.

Five thousand years ago, on a rise now known as Rink Hill at the meeting of the rivers Ettrick and Tweed, ancestors left us thousands of flakes of flint, flint cores, flint scrapers, and other worked tools, indicating long-time settlement. These generations of flint and stone knappers will have stood by the banks of the Tweed and Ettrick, and felt the same hidden powers as I did as a child.

Our ancestors may well have assumed this power to be that of river gods, or some other aspect of supernature. It is in our mindset to attribute natural phenomena to external agents: there must be a cause for what we experience, and if it cannot be seen, it must be imagined. This theory of agency is due to us being natural believers, believers in design and purpose, a mental remnant of successful evolution.

Hominins who heard a noise or who saw a twig move, and believed there was a bear in the cave or a wolf in the bush, were better at passing on their genes than hominins who did not believe. Those who investigated the cave or the bush, for food or through curiosity, they would be losers in evolution's biased lottery, that of natural selection. The lottery's bias being in favour of those whose genome furnished them with the aptitudes and attitudes which helped them survive the environment in which they lived by keeping their noses out of dangerous caves and bushes.

The force of the river torrent can move mud, sand, stones and boulders, and when in full flood, sometimes big boulders would shift position. Look at what is left on flood plains once floodwaters have receded. Look at the boulders which cover a river bed when the water is low. They are round, caused by eons of bashing other boulders and, in turn, being bashed. Each bash produces a pressure wave which, like sound, can move through the ground, and up through your feet, an infrasound you can feel but not hear, created by the percussion of big, rounded rocks striking each other on the river bed.

Abrasion, corrosion and attrition are terms applied to physical erosion in rivers, but traction, when boulders collide and clash, is the source of the primeval sensation of the powerful river gods. How many libations and votive offerings, over the eons, have been offered up to the gods and goddesses who reside in our rivers?

If you are sceptical of infrasound, imagine that you are a blind person who lived five hundred years ago, kidnapped and brought forward in time. You are standing on a kerbside where ten-ton trucks speed past. What would you hear and what you feel through you feet? And what would you think was the cause? Would you fall to your knees in fear, or would you raise your unseeing eyes to the heavens and pray?

Under the birch tree, the river gods were gone as the west wind weakened, but the trees still sang on, more hushed, a paean to Aeolus, the divine keeper of winds.

December 20th

A fungal foray round the garden was my fancy this morning, the pastime of choice after the first and failed attempt at the Scotsman crossword. The *Stropharia,* the Blue or Verdigris Roundhead, hadn't been examined for a few days, and there was now a new mushroom of a pretty blue-green hue, but impossible to clearly identify just like the last lot of Roundheads. These were still there, now a variety of colours none of which could remotely be described as green or blue. If this had been the first time that I had spotted them, I would never have identified them as *Stropharia.* Real mycologists need a microscope, and probably need to see the young, middle-aged and old fruiting bodies of the fungus.

With the feeling that mushroom identification was only ever going to be an inexact science for me, I found three examples of a red-brown toadstool growing almost within the canopy of the pine tree that shelters my siesta-seat. I'd obviously missed their emergence earlier in the week as they looked fairly mature. Their caps were a couple of inches across and they looked as if they had been bashed about a bit by either the weather or the wildlife. They could have been any one of a number of species and, given my experience with the changes in the *Stropharia,* I could only hazard a guess at naming them.

They seemed to match the description of the Rufous Milkcap, *Lactarius rufus. Lactarius* means 'milk-producing', indicating that an exudation is produced if the mushroom is damaged, and *rufus* means 'foxy-red': a foxy-red milk-producer sounds like a Jersey cow. I liked the portrayal of the Rufous Milkcap by Pat O'Reilly, of first-nature.com fame (see October 18th), where he writes that 'taste testing is an important step in identifying milkcap mushrooms, but for red-brown species such as this taste only a little piece or your tongue might explode!' This caught my attention and my imagination.

Against my usually conservative judgement on what I put in my mouth, I broke off a little piece of brown mushroom and placed it delicately on my tongue. There was nothing but a mild mushroom flavour. How disappointing! I didn't swallow, but kept the fragment stationary between my tongue and upper palette for a minute or two while I sat under the pine tree and had another go at the crossword.

Two clues later, I spat out the mush, with disdain at another failed mushroom identification. Another clue later, my mouth was burning as if I'd been eating fresh, green, chilli peppers. It took two hours for the sensation to slowly diminish, but I felt buoyed by a possible identification which had been promoted to probable, given that the Rufous Milkcap is often found beneath spruce, pine and birch trees, much like myself.

December 22nd

This could well be my favourite day of the year, celebrated for millennia, the winter solstice, the day when the back of the winter is broken. It will most likely get colder in the weeks to come but the psychological boost of increasing daylight holds promise. This cheers people up nowadays, so think what it must have been like over humanity's history when death lurked at the edge of darkness, only held at bay by the campfire.

Famine was waiting if hunting was poor or inadequate provision was made during the times of plenty. We live in a time of persistent plenty; for many of us, every day is a feast day, and darkness is a choice. This is the longest night of the year in the northern hemisphere so I thought I'd celebrate it by having a beer outside in the dark and cold, watching the moon.

A bottle of Jarl, from the appropriately named Fyne Ales brewery in Argyll, close to Loch Fyne, seemed like the very thing to tickle my palette while moon-watching. Jarl is a Norse word for 'chief', a top beer, certainly one of my favourites, of which I have many. I like beer. A light beer in nose, taste and alcohol content (3.8%), Jarl is a beautiful-to-look-at gold, with a citrus flavour and just a hint of summer grass. Wonderful slightly chilled, around 8°C on a hot summer's day, but still eminently quaffable on a cold night when it doesn't need cooled and can come straight off my beer shelf, which seldom gets above 10°C at this time of year.

When I retired, my colleagues in the science department got me a gift. The responsibility for buying this was given to colleague and pal, Michael (see November 18th). Michael's university degree was in brewing and one of his ex-classmates, Malcolm, is a brewer at Fyne Ales. Michael and, once or twice a year, Malcolm are temporary members, regular irregulars, of the Friday night church philosophy club at Cloisters. Michael procured for me a mixed case of twelve different bottles of beer from Fyne Ales and it could well be the best beer present which I have ever received. Only one of the beers was good; the rest were either very good or excellent. The Jarl was outstanding, and so it proved again as I sipped it and watched moonlit *Cumulus* clouds scud across the sky, lit by the moon which was still a few days from full.

Most folk can manage to put a name to the main phases of the moon, such as new moon, full moon, first quarter and third quarter. A bit counter-intuitive, as the 'quarters' are visually semicircles and sometimes called a 'half moon'. A lot of folk can also correctly name a crescent moon, that phase when the illuminated part of the moon is less than a quarter. Not so many folk know that when more than a quarter of the moon is illuminated, the phase is described as 'gibbous', from the Latin for 'humped'. If the 'hump' is getting smaller when the moon is heading to the 'third quarter', the moon is described as a 'gibbous moon waning'. Tonight, the humped moon was growing towards a full moon and is called a 'gibbous moon waxing', which to me sounds like a painful, hair-removal treatment you might suffer at a beauty salon and applied to your nether regions.

It is always good to try and view things from a different aspect, another point of view, but not just that of opinion. So long as you understand that the shiny bit of the moon is reflecting sunlight, it's a fun mental exercise to look at the moon and consider what Earth would look like if you were standing on the moon (see September 28th). What would you see? Would the Earth have phases like the moon? Take some time and think about this before you read on.

The moon orbits the earth once every 27 days and it rotates once on its axis every 27 days, so it seems to us on Earth as if the moon is not rotating because it always keeps the same side, the near side as we call it, pointing towards us. This is called synchronous rotation and is caused by something called tidal locking, a gravitational effect, which, you might be pleased to read, will not be discussed here. The far side of the moon is not 'the dark side of the moon' as it's sometimes called; it is just the side that we here on Earth never get a direct look at. When we see a dark, new moon, the far side, or 'the dark side of the moon', is fully lit by the sun.

If you were on the moon and wanted to view Earth, you would obviously need to position yourself on the side of the moon which faces Earth. From this position, the Earth would stay more or less stationary in the sky, other than a slight movement due to the moon's monthly shoogle, called libration, a perceived oscillation caused by the moon's orbit being elliptical rather than circular. Libration allows about 59% of the moon's surface to be seen from Earth, so the near side and the far side are unequal in size, if the far side is considered as the bit you never see.

Just like the moon, Earth also goes through a cycle of phases. As 27 days pass, you would see a full Earth, a gibbous Earth, a quarter Earth, a crescent Earth, a new Earth and so on. The big differences would be that the Earth doesn't move much in your lunar sky and the Earth's phases would be opposite to that of the moon as seen from Earth; when the moon was full to us here on Earth, there would be a new Earth from the perspective of someone on the moon; when the moon was a crescent, the Earth would be gibbous.

The Earth would look much bigger than the moon because the Earth's diameter would appear over three and a half times that of the moon, giving an apparent area ten times larger than the moon's. The moon is a dull lump of rock as its albedo, its ability to reflect light, is only a third that of Earth's. On average, the Earth reflects 37% of sunlight hitting it and the moon reflects 12%. So due to the greater size of the Earth and the difference in albedo, the Earth would appear much brighter, around thirty times brighter, than the moon. If the angles were just right, sunlight could reflect off one of Earth's oceans, flashing at an observer on the moon, just like the sun bounces off binoculars miles in the distance, as someone spies on you from the other side of a valley.

When a narrow, waxing crescent moon is observed, the rest of the near side of the moon is often dimly seen, described as 'the old moon in the new moon's arms'. This part of the moon is visible due to Earthshine, sunlight which has reflected off Earth towards the moon and is then reflected again, back towards Earth. Similar is seen with a narrow, waning crescent moon when the 'new moon is in the old moon's arms'. It is Earthshine which allows us to sometimes spot the new moon, manifesting itself as a dark circle in the sky, but not as dark as its surroundings. Time for another Jarl.

December 24th

We're off down the A701 to Moffat and my in-laws for Christmas. South out of Edinburgh, through Penicuik, towards Peebles, but turning right at Leadburn, we head for Moffat. As we pass Romano Bridge, the sunlight is angled perfectly to accentuate the cultivation terraces far to the left on a slope that was once a conifer plantation called Terrace Wood. There are a number of Iron Age settlements in the vicinity so these terraces may be over 2000 years old in origin, though some think they are medieval.

Iron Age people knew a good slope when they saw one and Border folk aren't stupid. It would be my guess that the terraces are Iron Age and were adapted and used many times over through the ages by Border people who preferred to farm on a west-facing slope, previously terraced, rather than on a boggy valley floor.

Down the road we go, through Blyth Bridge and on to the village of Broughton at the confluence of Biggar Water and the River Tweed. Broughton's chief claim to fame is that John Buchan, the 1st Baron Tweedsmuir and renowned author, spent much of his developmental years here, with his maternal grandparents, developing his love for the area. John Buchan's most well-known work is probably 'The Thirty-Nine Steps', a thriller set prior to the First World War and published in 1915, and which spawned film adaptations in 1935 by Alfred Hitchcock, 1959, 1978 and a 2008 version for television. Class has longevity.

Another of John Buchan's novels is 'Greenmantle', the sequel to 'The Thirty-Nine Steps' and the second of five novels featuring Richard Hannay, the novels' chief protagonist. This novel is the eponymous Greenmantle which gave its name to the flagship beer which launched the village of Broughton's other claim to fame, the Broughton Brewery, founded in 1979. You can see the brewery building clearly on the right of the road, opposite the primary school and play park, as you drive south through the village. Greenmantle is a brown, bittersweet ale, with a liquorice bouquet and smooth, hoppy aftertaste and, at 3.9% alcohol, a good session beer for a Friday night.

There is a long, straight bit of road a few miles south of Broughton where you can see the grass-covered ballast of a long-disused railway track. I'd noticed here on previous trips south with the open Tweed valley on the left and when the wind is from a south-westerly direction, you can experience an interesting effect if you open the car window. You will probably have unconsciously noticed this phenomenon, given it little thought, and then closed the window because some people find it irritating if not downright nauseating.

It's a sort of air-drumming, a whump-whump-whump sound called side-window buffeting or wind-throb. You feel it more than hear it; the pitch of the sound is so low that you feel it resonating in your chest and register it in your ears but without really hearing it. It helps to understand how this sensation manifests itself inside your head.

Sounds are pressure waves which vibrate the eardrum and these vibrations pass through the middle ear to the inner ear, where the movement is changed into a neurological signal in a snail-shaped structure called the cochlea. Infrasound, produced by side-window buffeting, stimulates the eardrum and middle ear but doesn't produce a neurological signal because the frequency of the vibration is below the threshold at which the cochlea can convert sound waves to neural signals.

The side-window buffeting is felt but not heard. As you normally hear sound when your eardrums vibrate, some people find this sensory dissonance quite unsettling. So how does side-window buffeting originate?

When a car window is opened, it disturbs the smooth airflow which moves over modern, streamlined cars. This smooth airflow becomes turbulent at the upstream edge of the open window. This causes an air-pressure vibration so the air pressure inside the car goes up and down. The resonance is usually infrasonic, of lower frequency than can be heard, and occupants feel a pulsating pounding as the air pressure oscillates.

The car interior has been transformed into a Helmholtz resonator, after the German physicist, Hermann von Helmholtz. The same effect is produced when you blow across the neck of an empty bottle, but the frequency of the vibration is usually at a higher pitch which is easily heard. Some musical instruments such as the ocarina are based on Helmholtz resonance.

So I opened the back window on the passenger side. Lynn was driving. The air was cold so Lynn was less than enamoured at my antics. I successfully managed to maximise the side-window buffeting effect by adjusting how wide the window was opened; it felt as if a helicopter was about to land on the car roof. At this point, I was threatened with violence which was, in my mind, uncalled-for, but nevertheless, discretion is sometimes the better part of valour, especially in maintaining sound marital relationships. I closed the car window. Some people are not very keen on learning about the science behind everyday occurrences.

We passed the Crook Inn and Tweedsmuir, where there is a turnoff for Talla Reservoir (more of that later) and followed the River Tweed, the road rising to the river's source at the head of the valley. Beyond the watershed, we came to the Devil's Beef Tub, a deep and dramatic, cauldron-shaped corrie formed by four hills. This corrie is one of the sources of the River Annan. It was described by Sir Walter Scott in his novel, Red Gauntlet, as looking

> '....as if four hills were laying their heads together to shut out daylight from the dark hollow space between them. A damned deep, black, blackguard-looking abyss of a hole it is'.

The Devil's Beef Tub got its strange name from the custom of the Border reivers hiding stolen cattle at the head of the Annan valley, combined with the cooking-pot shape of the glacier-carved corrie; the word 'corrie' comes from the Scottish Gaelic 'coire' meaning 'hollow' or 'cauldron'. At the risk of grammatical correctness, if, as some hold, the Border reivers are the 'Devils' in the Devil's Beef Tub, then the apostrophe is in the wrong place and the corrie should be the Devils' Beef Tub. However, if the said devil refers to the Lord of Annandale, the leader of the raiding reivers, then the apostrophe is correctly located in Devil's. When the muscles weaken, the breath comes in gasps and the sight dims, pedantry is one of the few pleasures left as one ages.

Wherever the apostrophe is placed, why should the Devil's (I'm sticking to convention) Beef Tub be such a great place to hide cattle, other than its remoteness? If you walk from Moffat towards the Tub, as it's colloquially called, the Tub cannot be seen. The valley looks like it comes to a smooth and gently sloped end five miles north of Moffat. If you had not driven past it and looked down into its depths on the way to Moffat, you would not credit that the Devil's Beef Tub was there.

So on down the windy way that is the A701, as it crosses the burns and becks which flow under the road to the River Annan on the valley floor below to the left, and on to Moffat. The A701 is joined by the B719 which leads over the rise to the right to the M74. Slightly less than half a mile further on, you come to a small bridge, hardly noticed as it looks more like a wall. This bridge crosses Gardenholm Linn, a burn that revealed dark secrets. These dark secrets were explicated by nascent forensic science to reveal a double murder.

On the 29th September, 1935, a woman found body parts by Gardenholm Linn. These were linked to the disappearance of Buck Ruxton's common-law wife and their housemaid from Lancaster. Ruxton was a doctor who did away with his wife, and the maid was perhaps unlucky enough to have witnessed some evidence of the crime so she was murdered as well. The bodies were butchered, parcelled up in thirty newspaper-wrapped packages, transported a hundred miles north and hidden by Gardenholm Linn. If Ruxton had realised the force with which a hillside burn can flow and how high it can rise when in flood, he might have made a better job of hiding the body parts and got away with the crime.

Ruxton was convicted on the back of evidence based on forensic entomology which identified maggots in the body remains and which allowed an estimation of the time of dumping based on the maggots' development; this gave a date of death. Forensic anthropology with the superimposition of a victim's photograph on an X-ray, fingerprint evidence and dental evidence helped secure Ruxton's conviction and signalled the importance of forensic science in the future of criminology. This case, these techniques and many other cases and techniques are detailed delightfully in Val McDermid's *'Forensics, The Anatomy of Crime'*: as she writes in her introduction, '...truth is stranger than fiction.'

Ruxton's trial ended on March 13th, 1936, with a 'guilty' verdict and Ruxton was sentenced to death. He was hanged on May 12th, 1936. The bridge over the picturesquely named Gardenholm Linn is known locally as Ruxton's Dump.

We drove through Moffat town centre, the Moffat Ram to the left, a statue by the famous Scottish sculptor, William Brodie. The same William Brodie also produced the Greyfriars Bobby Fountain on the corner of George IV Bridge and Candlemaker Row in Edinburgh.

The Moffat Ram was presented to the town in 1875 by William Colvin, a local businessman. At the unveiling, a local farmer pointed out that the ram 'hud nae lugs' (had no ears), much to the embarrassment of the artist Brodie. Moffat folklore has it that Brodie hung himself in disgrace. However, *'Mapping the Practice and Profession of Sculpture in Britain and Ireland 1851-1951'* has it that William Brodie died of heart disease in Edinburgh on October 30th,

1881, six years after the unveiling of the Moffat Ram; don't let facts get in the way of a good story.

On the other side of Moffat, just in time for lunch, we arrived to be greeted by John, Lynn's father, and his effervescent Cocker spaniel, Leah.

December 25th

With the Christmas morning festivities out of the way, I decided to visit an old friend whom I had encountered in late December, 1974, when I first visited Moffat to meet Lynn's family. My father-in-law, John, keeps a large, well maintained garden with many mature trees, any number of which could vie to be my favourite. But one is rather special, the biggest oak, a classic example of *Quercus robur, robur* meaning *'strong'* and *Quercus* the Latin for 'oak'. Some think the word *Quercus* comes from the Celtic, 'quer' meaning 'fine' and 'cuez' meaning 'tree'. My name for this fine tree is Big Oak.

Whatever the origin of its scientific name, this Big Oak has a girth of around sixteen feet, which equates to an age of about three hundred years. I've never been an overt tree-hugger but I can't help enjoying its scent and the texture of the gnarled bark against my cheek when I stretch my arms round its trunk; there is nothing wrong in being a closet tree-hugger. Three of me would be stretched to touch fingers round the circumference.

The tree looks out over the Annan valley to the south of Moffat, to an area called the Kerr, a word of Old Norse origin for 'marsh'. Big Oak grows on a river terrace that keeps much of its root system above the level of the River Annan's floodplain which, as the word floodplain suggests, is inclined to be rather wet, the water table never far from the surface, even in summer.

An estimation of the year 1715 would seem a reasonable guess for when Big Oak was an acorn, and it thrills and fascinates me to consider what this tree has inhaled, smelled and tasted over its time. Many people may be familiar with dendrochronology, the science of dating tree-rings in wooden artefacts and, at its most simple, counting the number of these growth rings to discern the age of a tree, one ring for each year of growth. Not so many people may be familiar with dendrochemistry.

During trees' normal processes of photosynthesis and respiration, in which chemicals are exchanged between the tree and its surroundings, trees also accumulate and store contaminants in their growth-rings. The basic idea behind dendrochemistry is that the annual growth-ring can act as a time-capsule of a tree's chemical environment during the year in which the growth-ring formed. Sampling can give information about the nature of the pollutants and, through the concentration of these pollutants, the level of pollution at that time. What history could this 300 year-old tree hold deep beneath its bark? Let's step back in tree-time.

There will be a ring, thirty rings into the oak, which holds evidence of radioactive rain. In 1986, at the Chernobyl Nuclear Power Plant in the Ukraine, a catastrophic nuclear accident occurred, releasing radioactive particles and gases which spread across Europe. Some of this fell on Scotland and the radioisotopes, caesium-137 and strontium-90, memorialise that event in this growth-ring. Both caesium-137 and strontium-90 have half-lives of around thirty years, so half of what was absorbed by the oak and laid down in that year's growth-ring will still be found there. In another thirty years, it will be down to a quarter of the initial concentration and, in further thirty years, down to an eighth, and so on.

I wonder, now and again, how many of Big Oak's rings hold records of blunders, disasters and sanctioned releases of radiation from our own Windscale nuclear site. Windscale was rechristened Sellafield in

1981 as part of a major reorganisation, but, in my mind, it was more a pointless public relations exercise in which bureaucrats and politicians seemed to think that erasing the Windscale name would expunge its faults and its managers' mistakes from the memories of the Britain and Ireland; Sellafield is less than eighty miles from the Irish coast.

The Windscale fire in 1957 was the worst nuclear accident in the UK's history, ranked in severity at level 5 on the International Nuclear Event Scale, level 7 being the worst possible. Between 1950 and 2000, there were another 20 serious incidents or accidents involving off-site radiological releases which warranted a rating on the International Nuclear Event Scale.

In addition, during the 1950s and 1960s there were protracted periods of known, deliberate discharges to the atmosphere of plutonium and uranium oxide particles. Does Big Oak have a little uranium or plutonium hiding fifty or sixty rings in from its bark?

Big Oak retains evidence of the detonation of the nuclear bombs on Hiroshima and Nagasaki. It holds records of nuclear weapons tests which were carried out throughout the second half of the 20th century to determine the effectiveness, yield, and explosive capability of similar weapons. Big Oak has history to tell.

Moffat was a spa town and in 1878 had its own 400-bedroom Moffat Hydropathic Hotel, the Moffat Hydro. This sadly burned down in 1921. Ailing tourists and hypochondriacs had to get to Moffat, so a short, spur, railway line was built between Moffat and Beattock in 1883. This line ceased carrying passengers in 1954 but continued for freight, before closing completely in 1964.

As these trains in the 1880s came into Moffat station, now Station Park, passengers will have looked west to the fine houses on the outskirts of Moffat and perhaps admired the majestic, then160 year-old, adolescent oak tree 200 yards to their left. They were unlikely to have imagined that the fuel which powered their journey would leave a memory, for over eighty years of these trains running, of the train-fuels' combustion products, heavy metals and hydrocarbons, within the trunk of that tall, elegant, young oak.

Vesuvius erupted on seventeen occasions between 1715 and the present day. Has Big Oak kept account of these eruptions, and of those of countless other volcanoes? If the wind on a certain day was blowing the wrong way so that Big Oak has no record of a particular eruption, then you can be sure that there are other big oaks around the world which retain these records. The next time you see a Yule log burning at Christmas time, bear in mind that it is not only the wooden log that is going up in smoke, but the historical log chemically memorialised in its growth-rings.

The effervescent Leah's barking and Lynn's call, wondering where I was hiding in the garden and why I was being antisocial, brought me out from my reverie. Excuses that I was being very social and communing with an old friend cut me little slack with Lynn. Leah seemed to understand, raising one eyebrow as some dogs do: maybe some of her friends are trees.

December 26th

Before our return trip to Edinburgh, I wanted to bid Big Oak adieu, not in any sentimental way, but just because I like a walk round John's garden and, in a way, it's rather ceremonial, given that this is my forty-second Christmas in Moffat. The oak tree has been a symbol of veneration in cultures across Europe from Greece to Scandinavia, and our own Celtic pagans have held the oak tree sacred for over two and a half thousand years. There are other oaks in the garden but they do not project Big Oak's magnificence. They are likely offspring of Big Oak, or siblings, even though some may be a hundred years younger. Tree-time is longer than human-time, which is usually referred to as time because people seldom think on any time scale that is alien to their immediate self-importance.

Time, and the effects that ensue with its passing, can only be appreciated when you throw off the shackles of self-absorption and realise that there are different types of time during which our human significance diminishes as the time scales increase. Beyond the human-time scale of our petty lives, in increasing scale are tree-time, historical time, archaeological time, evolutionary time, geological time and astronomical time. There are links between these ranges: palaeontology, the study of our fossil past, represents the overlap between geological time and evolutionary time; comets and asteroids impacting the early earth link geological time and astronomical time.

Don't just think bigger and longer. There is ephemeral time during which organisms come into existence, reproduce and die in the space of a day; and then there is microbial time, which, as microbes mutate and adapt, demonstrates that evolutionary time eclipses all lesser scales. Could it be, given similarities in time at different scales, that there is a fractal aspect to time? Fractals are patterns which exhibit similarity at ever decreasing or increasing scale, such as in river networks, the branching in trees and in coastlines when viewed from above with differing magnification from the macroscopic to the microscopic.

The oak trees in the garden are all within tens of metres of each other and there is now evidence that such an arboreal community not only communicates amongst its members, but that these members mutually support each other. When a tree is attacked by a herbivore, it can, in minutes, produce toxins which the consumer finds unpalatable. The tree also releases warning chemicals to tell other trees, of their own species, that herbivores are hungry, so they should pre-emptively start making the nasty-tasting toxins before they are attacked.

Trees, especially oak trees, are very good at forming symbiotic, mutually beneficial, relationships with fungi, and millions of years of concurrent evolution ensures reciprocal benefits. If you indulge in gardening, at some time, you will have came across a network of thin, white fibres in the soil. This is a fungal structure called the mycelium, a mass of branching thread-like hyphae. In relationships with trees, fungal threads of mycorrhiza, or the fungus 'roots', extend through the soil and penetrate into tree roots. Fungi are unable to photosynthesise so they get their carbohydrates from the trees to fuel their growth. The trees, in return, get nitrogen and phosphorus from the fungi which extract these nutrients from the soil: nitrogen and phosphorus are essential to the trees' health but are often in short supply.

After a fungus envelopes a tree's roots, it can then grow through the soil widening the tree's scope until the fungus links with fungi from the roots of other trees, creating a chemical communication network. Trees can share information about herbivorous attacks not only by air but by underground connection, and it is not difficult to understand the benefits of this evolutionary adaption.

Any gas-alert released by a tree to warn its community of assault would be prone to the vagaries of the weather; trees upwind would get no warning. Underground transmission of information may be slower but would have 360° effectiveness. When members of a tribe are under threat, they appreciate alerts, and they also appreciate any spare food if they are short and others have a surplus. In times of stress, trees help each other by transferring food chemicals from efficient photosynthesisers to the less efficient members of their community, by way of the underground, fungal, transport system.

These tree stories and many others are elegantly told and elaborated on in Peter Wohlleben's *'The Hidden Life of Trees, What they feel, How they communicate'*. Since reading this book, I have come to regard trees, not so much as woods and forests, but more as families and as diverse communities. Peter Wohlleben has written a book that has compelled me to see trees in a new light with fresh eyes.

In 1816, known as 'The Year without a Summer', the year after the eruption of Mount Tambora, a volcano in the Dutch East Indies, there were major food shortages across the Northern Hemisphere due to lower light levels resulting in decreased crop yields. Could Big Oak, a strong community member, have aided its younger kin and help maintain them during such times when isolated individuals might have struggled, without such social security as Big Oak's aid? I like to think so. We have much to learn from trees, but not just in the protection of the weaker members of our societies.

December 31st

Like those before it, Storm Frank has come and gone. I thought a doddle round the garden would let me assess the requirement for any remedial action, but I found that Storm Frank had been a bit under the weather when blowing across Edinburgh. He had been more destructive further south; the Scottish Borders and the north of England bore the brunt of Frank's fury. With sympathies for the south, what I thought would have been a post-Storm Frank clean-up was replaced with an end of year review of what was providing colour in the mid-winter garden.

Two bellflowers were still showing blue, *Campanula portenschlagiana* and *Campanula poscharskyana*. *Campanula* means 'little bell' as campanologists should know, or at the very least it should ring a bell. The species names are derived from people whose names are difficult to pronounce, an Austrian naturalist, Franz von Portenschlag-Leydermayer and a German gardener, Gustav Poscharsky. I prefer the alternative name for the first of the two, which is *Campanula muralis,* as that explains where it's often found, growing on walls, its common name the Wall Bellflower. The second is also often found growing up or down walls as its common name, the Trailing Bellflower, implies.

The pink *Schizostylis coccinea* is well past its best, its last few flowers on the tip of their stems stretching up for the last sunbeams of December. Both the *Viburnums* in the front garden are going strong. *Viburnum farreri* and *Viburnum bodnantense* have held on to their flowers and their scent, which Storm Frank failed to blow away. The periwinkle in the back garden has a few flowers of a pretty blue hue which could be either periwinkle blue by definition, but I'm inclined to view it as lavender blue as the petals are a little faded. Lavender blue or periwinkle blue is a bit pedantic as they are almost identical in some colour-definition schemes.

Smidgeons of yellow dot the back garden like little yellow butterflies. This is due to Winter Jasmine bushes, one either side of the back grass/moss, two golden hygrocybes which are pushing through that moss, and two Tête-á-Tête daffodils which have decided to jump the gun and not to wait for their pot-mates before blooming.

Some berries still await avian attack and they announce their presence with visual aplomb. The orange berries of the Stinking Iris, *Iris foetidissima*, brighten dull corners like a small child's smile brightens a dark mood. Snowberries shine white in the sun but look as unappetising as ever which explains why, despite the toxins they carry, cases of poisoning are seldom seen in casualty wards. The cotoneasters are, at the moment, the blackbirds' first choice for berry-feasts now that the rowan trees are bare.

Cotoneaster frigidus, the Tree Cotoneaster, is festooned with arched branches laden with rich-red clusters of berries. This medium sized tree is often ignored by birds until January (tomorrow!) when more-appetising fare has been scoffed, but this year, wood pigeons sit on the topmost arches clearing them of fruit while assorted migrant thrushes, and our own indigenous birds, hang on the lower branches gorging themselves. Some years, apples and plums produce more flavoursome fruit than other years, and the same may be true of the Tree Cotoneaster, but I shall never know because *Cotoneaster* species contain cyanogenic glycosides, so all parts of them are potentially poisonous.

As the name *frigidus* suggests, this tree thrives in cold climates; it hails from the Himalayas. Its large inflorescences of creamy white flowers attract lots of pollinating insects in the summer, so it is a useful plant to have in the garden. *Cotoneaster frigidus* can tolerate air pollution, deep shade and dry conditions, so if you are looking for a moderately-sized tree, which won't dwarf a moderately-sized house, that feeds pollinators in the summer and birds in the winter, with the added benefit of being pleasing on the eye, then this is the tree for you. I don't have one but I don't really mind as it is very common throughout the Grange so I can appreciate it when I wander and ponder on my way to the shops in Marchmont.

'In the depths of winter I finally learned that within me there lay an invincible summer.'

Albert Camus (1913-1960)

Appendices

Fungi

Some of the fungi discussed in the *Going Nowhere Slow* trilogy:

Auricularia auricula-judae, Jelly Ear---December 17th

Calocybe gambosa, St. George's Mushroom---May 29th

Clavulinopsis helvola, Yellow Club fungus---November 8th

Clavulinopsis luteoalba, Apricot Club fungus---November 8th

Galerina sp, Helmets---November 15th

Hygrocybe ceracea, Butter Waxcap---October 18th

Hygrocybe chlorophana, Golden Waxcap---November 8th

Hygrocybe coccinea, Scarlet Waxcap---October 18th

Hygrocybe quieta, Oily Waxcap, Tranquil Waxcap---December 6th

Lactarius rufus, Rufous Milkcap---December 20th

Marasmius oreades, Fairy Ring Mushroom---November 11th

Mycena sp, Bonnets---November 15th

Panaeolina foenisecii, Brown Mottlegill, Mower's Mushroom---October 19th

Podosphaera mors-uvae, American Gooseberry Mildew---August 8th

Psilocybe Mexicana, Mexican Liberty Cap, Teonanacatl---October 18th

Psilocybe semilanceata, Liberty Cap, Magic Mushroom---October 18th

Rhizoctonia solani, Black scurf---November 24th

Stropharia aeruginosa, Verdigris Roundhead---December 6th

Stropharia caerulea, Blue Roundhead---December 6th

Plants

Some of the plants discussed in the *Going Nowhere Slow* trilogy:

Aesculus hippocastanum, Horse chestnut---June 9th

Allium ursinum, Wild garlic, ramsons, wood garlic---May 14th

Artemisia dracunculus, French Tarragon---July 25th

Artemesia dracunculoides, Russian Tarragon---July 25th

Arum maculatum, Lords-and-ladies, priest's pintle, arum lily---July 16th

Atropa belladonna, Belladonna, deadly nightshade---August 16th

Betula papyrifera, Paper Bark Birch---March 5th

Betula pendula, Silver Birch---March 5th

Betula pubescens, Downy Birch---March 5th

Betula utilis, Himalayan Birch---January 18th

Brassica oleracea, Brussels sprout---August 21st

Campanula portenschlagiana or *muralis*, Wall Bellflower---December 31st

Campanula poscharskyana, Trailing Bellflower---December 31st

Cedrus deodara, Deodar, Himalayan Cedar---January 5th

Clematis tangutica, Golden clematis---July 14th

Colchicum autumnale, Autumn crocuses, Meadow Saffron, Naked Ladies---November 3rd

Convallaria majalis, Lily-of-the valley---May 14th

Corydalis lutea, Yellow Fumitory, Yellow Corydalis---December 15th

Cotoneaster frigidus, Tree Cotoneaster---December 31st

Crocus vernus, Spring Crocus---March 2nd

Crocus sativus, Saffron Crocus---March 2nd

Cytisus scoparius, Common, or Scotch, Broom---August 25th

Digitalis purpurea, Foxglove---June 22nd

Eranthis hyemalis, Winter Aconite---January 25th

Erica carnea, Winter-flowering heather---January 3rd

Galanthus nivalis, Snowdrops---January 19th

Galium aparine, Sticky willy, cleavers, goosegrass---July 10th

Hesperantha coccinea, Crimson Flag, African lily---October 14th

Hyacinthoides hispanica, Spanish bluebell---May 5th

Hyacinthoides non-scripta, Common bluebell---May 5th

Hyacinthoides × *massartiana*, bluebell hybrid---May 5th

Hydrangea macrophylla, Mophead /Lacecap hydrangeas---December 11th

Ilex aquifolium, Common holly---June 9th

Iris foetidissima, Stinking iris, Gladdon---November 30th

Iris reticulata, Netted iris---February 6th

Lychnis coronaria, Rose campion---July 14th

Kerria japonica, Kerria, bachelor's buttons---April 12th

Magnolia × *soulangeana*, Saucer Magnolia---April 19th

Malus domestica or *pumila,* apple 'James Grieve'---October 23rd

Picea breweriana, Brewer's Spruce, Weeping Spruce---February 22nd

Pieris floribunda, Forest Flame---April 3rd

Pinus nigra, Black Pine---January 12th

Pinus sylvestris, Scots pine---September 3rd

Prunus subhirtella, Winter-flowering Cherry---January 5th

Populus trichocarpa, Western Balsam Poplar---November 22nd

Quercus robur, Common Oak, European Oak---December 25th

Ribes grossularia, Gooseberry---January 15th

Ribes nigrum, Black currant---January 15th

Ribes sanguineum, Flowering Currant---February 15th

Rosmarinus officinalis, Rosemary---April 29th

Solanum tuberosum, potato cultivar 'Pink Fir Apple'---November 7th

Schizostylis coccinea, Crimson Flag, African lily---October 14th

Symphoricarpos albus, Common Snowberry---December 15th

Taxus baccata, Common, or European, Yew---August 11th

Taxus brevifolia, Pacific yew---August 11th

Tilia vulgaris, Tilia × *europaea*, Common lime, Linden---December 7th

Trifolium repens, White Clover---July 1st

Urtica dioica, Common nettle, stinging nettle---July 3rd

Viburnum x *bodnantense*, Arrowwood---October 8th

Viburnum farreri, Farrer viburnum---October 8th

Viburnum lantana, Wayfarer tree---October 8th

Viburnum opulus, Guelder rose---October 8th

Vinca major, Greater periwinkle---November 24th

Vinca minor, Lesser periwinkle---November 24th

Animals

Some of the animals discussed in the *Going Nowhere Slow* trilogy:

Aegithalos caudatus, Long-tailed tit---November 5th

Acanthosoma haemorrhoidale, Hawthorn Shieldbug---August 8th

Aglais Io, Peacock butterfly---April 20th

Andrena scotica, Chocolate mining bee---May 17th

Anthocoris nemorum, Flower bug, berry bug---September 4th

Apus apus, Common swift---July 23rd

Bombus distinguendus, Great Yellow Bumblebee---August 4th

Bombus hypnorum, Tree bumblebee---May 4th

Bombus lapidarius, Red-tailed bumblebee---March 15th

Bombus lucorum, White-tailed bumblebee---April 7th

Bombus pascuorum, Common carder bee---April 10th

Bombus pratorum, Early (-nesting) bumblebee---April 10th

Bombus terrestris, Buff-tailed bumblebee---March 8th

Carduelis spinus, Siskin---June 23rd

Chloris chloris, Greenfinch---November 8th

Columba livia, Rock pigeon, rock dove---June 13th

Columba livia domestica, Domestic pigeon---June 13th

Columba palumbus, Wood Pigeon---December 4th

Cornu aspersum, Common, or brown, garden snail---May 21st

Corvus corax, Raven---October 12th

Corvus corone, Carrion Crow---February 12th

Corvus monedula, Jackdaw---June 18th

Crataerina pallida, Common Swift Louse Fly---July 23rd

Delia radicum, Cabbage root fly---August 21st

Dendrocopos major, Great spotted woodpecker---January 1st

Erithacus rubecula, Robin Redbreast---February 24th

Haliaeetus albicilla, White-tailed sea-eagle---July 31st

Megachile sp, Leafcutter bee---May 17th

Meligethes aeneus, Common pollen beetle---April 19th

Nematus ribesii, Gooseberry sawfly---May 18th

Pareas iwasakii, Iwasaki's snail-eater snake---May 21st

Philaenus spumarius, Froghopper---June 28th

Pieris brassicae, Cabbage white butterfly---August 21st

Prunella modularis, Dunnock, Hedge Accentor, Hedge Sparrow---February 28th

Pyrrhalta viburni, Viburnum beetle---June 17th

Pyrrhula pyrrhula, Bullfinch---February 14th

Sciurus carolinensis, Grey squirrel---October 12th

Troglodytes troglodytes Wren---January 24th

Turdus merula, Blackbird---January 17th

Vulpes vulpes, Red fox---November 1st

Websites

Some of the websites discussed within the *Going Nowhere Slow* trilogy and which have enhanced my life during the researching, drafting and writing of it:

www.newscientist.com I have been reading New Scientist magazine since I first picked it up in the coffee lounge of the chemistry department in St Andrews University in 1974. Just as the magazine has informed and inspired me for over four decades, the website can do the same for current and future generations of scientists, science teachers and anyone with an interest in things scientific.

---October 18th www.first-nature.com

---November 3rd www.thepoisongarden.co.uk

---January 1st www.bto.org The British Trust for Ornithology

---February 10th www.cloudappreciationsociety.org

---February 15th www.compoundchem.com

---March 30th www.atoptics.co.uk Atmospheric optics

---May 4th www.bumblebeeconservation.org

---May 4th www.bwars.com Bees, Wasps and Ants Recording Society (BWARS)

---June 8th www.wmocloudatlas.org World Meteorological Organization

---June 18th www.wiktionary.org

---July 31st www.orkneyjar.com An extensive exploration of the ancient history, folklore and traditions of Orkney

Books

Some of the books discussed within the *Going Nowhere Slow* trilogy and which have enhanced my life during the researching, drafting and writing of it:

--- August 27th Anil Ananthaswamy, *'The Man Who Wasn't There: Tales from the Edge of the Self'*

--- October 1st Walter Elliot, *'Selkirkshire and The Borders, A personal view of the archaeology and history as seen by Walter Elliot, Book One, From the Beginning of Time to AD 1603'*

--- November 6th Robert Macfarlane, *'Landmarks'*

--- December 7th Donald Pigott, *'Lime'* in *'A Handbook of Scotland's Trees, the essential guide for enthusiasts, gardeners and woodland lovers to species cultivation, habits, uses and lore'*, edited by Fi Martynoga for Reforesting Scotland

--- December 24th Val McDermid, *'Forensics, The Anatomy of Crime'*

--- December 26th Peter Wohlleben, *'The Hidden Life of Trees, What they feel, How they communicate'*

--- January 29th Andrea Wulf, *'The Invention of Nature: The Adventures of Alexander von Humboldt, the Lost Hero of Science'*

--- February 6th Richard Mabey, *'The Ash and the Beech'*

--- February 10th Gavin Pretor-Pinney, *'The Cloudspotter's Guide'*

--- February 12th Esther Woolfson, *'Corvus, A Life with Birds'*

--- March 17th Giulia Enders, *'Gut: the inside story of our body's most under-rated organ'*

--- March 17th <u>Erica and Justin Sonnenberg</u>, *'The Good Gut: Taking Control of Your Weight, Your Mood, and Your Long-Term Health'*

--- April 10th <u>Dave Goulson</u>, *'A Sting in the Tale'*

--- April 20th <u>Peter Forbes</u>, *'Dazzled and Deceived, Mimicry and Camouflage'*

--- April 24th <u>Gavin Pretor-Pinney</u>, *'The Wavewatcher's Companion'*

--- April 29th <u>Ben-Erik van Wyk and Michael Wink</u>, *'Phytomedicines, Herbal Drugs, and Poisons'*

--- May 5th <u>Fred Pearce</u>, *'The New Wild: Why invasive species will be nature's salvation'*

--- May 21st <u>Helen Scales</u>, *'Spirals in Time, The Secret Life and Curious Afterlife of Seashells'*

--- June 22nd <u>John Wright</u>, 'A Natural History of the Hedgerow: and ditches, dykes and dry stone walls'

--- July 7th <u>Lone Frank</u>, 'My Beautiful Genome: Exposing Our Genetic Future, One Quirk at a Time'

--- July 18th <u>Richard Mabey</u>, *'The Cabaret of Plants: Botany and the Imagination'*

--- August 3rd <u>David Miles</u>, *'The Tale of the Axe: How the Neolithic Revolution Transformed Britain'*

Often and valuably visited but not discussed within the *Going Nowhere Slow* trilogy:

<u>A.T. Johnson and H.A. Smith</u>, *'Plant Names Simplified: Their Pronunciation, Derivation and Meaning'*

Beers

A few of the beers discussed within the *Going Nowhere Slow* trilogy and which have enhanced my life during the researching, drafting and writing of it:

--- December 18th *Ritual*, the Alchemy Brewery in Livingston

--- December 22nd *Jarl,* the Fyne Ales brewery in Argyll

--- December 24th *Greenmantle,* the Broughton Brewery

--- January 18th *Schiehallion*, the Harviestoun Brewery at Alva in Clackmannanshire

--- February 6th *Rauchbier,* the German smoked beer made in Bamberg

--- March 4th *Ghost Ship*, the Adnams Brewery in Southwold in Suffolk

--- May 1st *Edelstoff*, the Augustiner Brewery in Bavaria

 --- May 1st *Lagerbier Hell*, the Augustiner Brewery in Bavaria

--- May 16th *Pilsner Urquell*, the Pilsner Urquell Brewery in Pilsen, Czech Republic

--- July 18th *Primátor Premium Lager,* the Nachod Brewery in the Czech Republic

--- July 29th *Yellowhammer*, the Black Isle Brewery

--- July 29th *Red Kite,* the Black Isle Brewery

--- July 30th *Island Hopping,* the Swannay Brewery, Orkney

--- August 4th *Scapa Special*, the Swannay Brewery, Orkney

--- August 4th   *Dark Island,* the Orkney Brewery, Orkney

The *Going Nowhere Slow* trilogy

Going Nowhere Slow: Autumn into Winter, covers August 17th to December 31st, 2015.

Going Nowhere Slow: *Winter into Spring*, covers January 1st to April 29th, 2016.

Going Nowhere Slow: Spring into Summer, covers May 1st to August 17th, 2016.

January

'January is here, with eyes that keenly glow,
A frost-mailed warrior
striding a shadowy steed of snow.'

Edgar Fawcett (1847-1904)

'To read a poem in January is as lovely as to go for a walk in June.'

Jean-Paul Sartre (1905-1980)

'The sun came out,
And the snowman cried.
His tears ran down
on every side.
His tears ran down
Till the spot was cleared.
He cried so hard
That he disappeared.'

Margaret Hillert (1920-2014)

January 1st

One of my ornithological excitements last summer was the visit of a Great Spotted Woodpecker to the back garden. It would climb up, down and round the big pear tree at the bottom of the garden, tapping on flakes of bark and looking for the wee beasties that are part of its diet, in addition to seeds and nuts. Cute, the Great Spotted Woodpecker may be, but it will eat other birds' eggs if it gets the chance, which is regarded by some people as uncute. However, *Dendrocopos major* hits the cute-buttons for me, especially as it was a first-footer, a New Year visitor today.

Dendro-copos means 'tree-cutter' and the *major* lets you differentiate between the Great Spotted Woodpecker and the Lesser Spotted Woodpecker, *Dendrocopos minor,* which, after DNA studies in 2015, was renamed *Dryobates minor, Dryo-bates* being the 'wood-walker'.

These two black and white, with a bit of red on the head, woodpeckers are not difficult to tell apart. The Great version is about the size of a blackbird and the Lesser bird is around two thirds the length and a quarter of the weight of its larger Great cousin, closer to the size of a sparrow. Males and juveniles of both birds have red on the head but females do not. There are around 1500 pairs of the Lesser Spotted Woodpecker in Britain, whereas there are about 140,000 pairs of the Great Spotted Woodpecker, so you'll be pretty lucky to spot the smaller of the two species.

The recent story of the Great Spotted Woodpecker population is a positive one. In the last fifteen years, the Scottish population has tripled, so it shouldn't surprise me that I've had a visitor to my garden; but it does still thrill and excite me. I love watching it play hide-and-seek. If it's there in the garden first and it spots me enter, it flies away. If I'm in the garden first and the woodpecker flies in and notices me, it hides behind the trunk of the tree on which it has landed. It goes about its business, peeks at me from behind the trunk, retreats before glancing round the other side of the trunk to see if I'm still there; I may be a threat. It doesn't mind my stationary presence but if I try to move to a better position for observing the bird, it's off.

Last summer's Great Spotted Woodpecker had a crimson cap, but my New Year first-footer, today, had a black cap with a crimson neck-guard at the back. My initial thought was that I'd had two visitors of the same species, but as juvenile Great Spotted Woodpeckers have a red crown to their head and mature males a red nape to their neck, my suspicions are that they are one in the same bird, the juvenile having gained its adult plumage in the autumn. The female Great Spotted Woodpecker is less ostentatious with a distinctly monochrome head and upper body.

The behaviour of my New Year guest also fuelled my suspicions that this was the same woodpecker because the summer youngster and this adult followed the same modus operandi. They would land in the apple tree, play hide-and-seek with me, go to the peanut bird feeder, to hang from the bottom of it using its tail as a support prop. Both birds would then carefully extract a single peanut using its long, sharp bill with the delicate accuracy of an ophthalmic surgeon removing an iron filing from an unfortunate metal-worker's eye. They would then fly off to the same sycamore tree in a neighbour's garden before returning ten minutes later to repeat the performance. I was privileged to be in the front stalls.

Why the Great Spotted Woodpecker should be increasing its numbers is not as easily answered as you might think. Any change in population density of an organism these days is immediately accredited to, in the case of a positive change, or blamed on, in the case of a negative change, global warming. The territorial boundaries of plant and animal populations generally move north in the northern hemisphere and south in the southern hemisphere as average temperatures rise. Increased Scottish population of Great Spotted Woodpeckers could support this hypothesis, but the science does not.

At its website (www.bto.org), The British Trust for Ornithology announces,

> 'The British Trust for Ornithology (BTO) is an independent charitable research institute combining professional and citizen science aimed at using evidence of change in wildlife populations, particularly birds, to inform the public, opinion-formers and environmental policy- and decision-makers.'

It is a treasure trove of avian jewels of information, easily accessible for the mildly curious bird-watcher and, with a little mouse-clicking, there is a huge nest of knowledge for the more serious ornithologist. According to the BTO, the main reason for the last two decades' increase in Great Spotted Woodpecker numbers has been the decline in starlings, which compete with Great Spotted Woodpecker for nest sites. Without the BTO, how would I have ever known this?

Anyone with the slightest interest in finding out about birds should use this well designed and attractive website as a first port of call, then follow the links to a cornucopia of further information and peer-reviewed papers for more depth and entertainment.

January 3rd

The winter-flowering heather, *Erica carnea*, normally starts to show its colours in January and this year is no exception, the buds breaking slightly earlier than usual. *Erica* means 'heath' or 'heather', but *carnea* is interesting. It is derived from the Latin, 'carnis' meaning 'of the flesh', of pink colouration. 'Carnis' also gives us carnivorous, carnage, carnal, carnation (pink flower); and my favourite, carnival, from 'carne' and 'vale', the Latin 'goodbye', through Italian, 'carnevale' and the French, 'carnaval', meaning, 'O flesh, farewell!' Celebrate and never mind the consequences.

Perhaps you are a carnophobe and have a fear or an aversion to a meat diet and even the sight of meat causes you nausea? Have you ever been described as 'the devil incarnate', or do you believe in reincarnation? The least said about carnophilia the better.

January 5th

Once again, the layer of grey *Stratus* cloud is so thick that the detectors at the back-door think it's dark and switch on the security light when I walk outside at 11o'clock in the morning. The wind was coming from an easterly direction with the chill of the North Sea behind it. Damp winds seem to be able to pass on this chill much more effectively than dry winds, even when the temperature is the same. This damp chill can be defeated by wearing the right clothes and it helps if you understand the principles of insulation, heat retention and heat loss. Every country has a meteorological philosopher who has came up with some version or other of the old chestnut, 'There's no such thing as bad weather, only unsuitable clothing', particularly in countries where you have to wear clothes to keep warm and dry.

Your winter woollies are wonderfully warm on frosty, dry days but seem insufficient on damp days with the temperature is just above freezing. Natural fibres like wool and cotton have microscopic gaps in them, normally occupied by air, a good heat insulator, so they keep you nice and warm when it's cold and dry. On dank days, wool and cotton readily absorb moisture from the air filling these microscopic gaps. As your woollies absorb more moisture, their insulating ability declines as water replaces the air, reducing the insulating capacity of the clothing, thus causing you to feel colder.

Cotton makes comfortable clothing as, like wool, it has the capacity to absorb moisture and it also has good heat insulation properties due to its air-spaces between and within its fibres. The molecular structure of the cellulose, from which cotton is constructed, is attractive to water, as chemical connections called hydrogen bonds form between the cellulose and the water molecules. If you don't like chemistry, then the water 'sticks' to the cellulose. When you wear cotton next to your skin and you get a little sweaty, water molecules can move into these air-spaces and again, like wool, the cotton loses its insulation. This keeps you comfortable on slightly sweaty days but can cause problems during cold weather when wool and cotton get wet through sweat or rain, and hypothermia can become a risk in hiking and hill-climbing contexts.

In these situations, synthetics such as polyester are preferred as the next-to-skin layer because its fibres are solid, and any water is weakly absorbed so does not 'stick' to the fibre surface. This allows such synthetics to wick water away from the skin by capillary action, all the while retaining their insulation ability due to air-pockets between the fibres remaining water-free. This is the concept behind 'breathable' fabrics.

Cotton can absorb, by % weight, about 15 times more water on and within its fibres than polyester. This explains why washed synthetics dry so much faster than washed cotton or wool which can seem to take ages to dry.

So if you feel the cold on damp days, wear a waterproof with insulating synthetics underneath. When it's nice and warm, cotton is a comfortable cloth to wear as it absorbs your sweatiness (up to a point) and leaves you feeling dry.

I donned my waterproof and insulating under-layer before setting off at a brisk pace up Dick Place. I carried on through Marchmont to the Meadows, to see if I could spot any interesting, unseasonal effects due to the funny winter. I also like to look at trees against the neutral background of a grey, leaden sky. Detail which is lost against a bright, blue sky or a white, sunlit cloudscape can become apparent on dull days.

Halfway along Dick Place, the first joy that I encountered was a Winter-flowering Cherry, *Prunus subhirtella; Prunus* being the classic name for the flowering and fruiting plums and cherries, and *subhirtella* means 'slightly hairy', pertaining to the leaves and young wood. The Winter-flowering Cherry normally produces flowers from November through to March, mild conditions encouraging more bloom. This twelve-foot specimen was covered in small, white flowers, in a profusion which I had never previously seen in January.

Another Winter-flowering Cherry was showing off in Marchmont Crescent, but the best to be seen was in the upper half of Findhorn Place. This magnificent example was competing with a *Viburnum bodnantense,* probably variety 'Dawn', which was holding its own with its pink and white clusters of blossom. The flowering cherry edged the competition due to its greater size: shrubs and trees are like rugby players, a good, big one has the advantage over a good, little one

Another tree that enthrals me, and does so every time I pass it, is a *Cedrus deodara*, a Deodar, or Himalayan Cedar, in Dick Place. This huge example should be totally out of place in a front garden but, in reality, dominates the street as if it has been there for longer than the house to which it belongs, unlikely to be the case. Deodar derives from the ancient Sanskrit meaning 'wood of the Gods' and forests of Deodar were Hindu sacred places of worship and meditation.

Alaister Scott was a man who loved trees and was their friend and protector. He wrote in *'Trees in the Grange'* (see December 7th), presumably tongue in cheek, that children brought up where there is a big Deodar to climb may be better than the rest of humanity, which may or may not be the case, but this demonstrates the esteem in which Alaister held the Deodar. Alaister was brought up in Jedburgh and spent a lot of time climbing trees as a boy, before a career in forestry, and he obviously understood people as well as he understood trees. The Deodar, native to the western Himalayas, is the sort of tree that could grace the courtyard of a Shaolin Temple or a garden of a Chinese emperor, and the specimen which I adore brings a certain majesty to Dick Place.

January 8th

The first real hoar frost of the year had painted the back grass a grey-white which twinkled where it caught the sun. Late in the morning, I ventured out to the siesta-seat to see if conditions were comfortable enough for a coffee in the sharp light.

As the air temperature had risen through the morning, the grass had started to thaw from the top down. The tufts of grass, three to four inches high, which had grown slowly over the winter, stood proud of the still frozen moss below. The moss was an unappetising, yellow slime-green whereas the grass above looked verdant and healthy. If I were a horse which could think, the thought that spring was on the horizon would probably be going through my equine mind. Of course, if I were a thoughtful horse, I would know not to eat the yummy-looking grass or I could risk a bout of laminitis, a disease which could make my hooves tender.

Grass that stops growing due to cold temperatures cannot metabolise sugars to make the starch which is produced when the temperature is higher. Sugar in pasture grass during winter isn't used by the plant as fast as it is produced, so sugar accumulates in the grass. If horses are allowed to eat this cold-weather grass, they risk laminitis. Sugars cause an increase in insulin levels, and this is the trigger for laminitis, not a disease of the hoof but tender hooves being a symptom. Laminitis is a metabolic disease, akin to type 2 diabetes. Both diseases involve insulin resistance.

January 11th

The squirrels are particularly frolicsome, probably a preamble to mating which usually occurs for grey squirrels during January and February. A successful frolic might produce a litter of between two and five kits six weeks later. In a good year for squirrels, the process is repeated in May or June.

Five squirrels have been jumping about the garden, rolling, chasing, using bushes, trees and garden furniture in their own sciurine (squirrely) version of free-running. Free-running is that athletic, acrobatic and aesthetic pursuit where practitioners move through the urban environment with speed, fluidity and grace, as much a form of freedom of expression as a sport. The squirrels are good at this, which I regard as free entertainment, especially when a bit of magpie-chasing is included. One brave squirrel tried harassing a wood pigeon but was met with casual indifference bordering on disdain. The pigeon fronted up to the squirrel which opted for a philosophy of retreat with dignity maintained, suggesting that the squirrel had previously encountered moody wood pigeons, ones with attitude like this one.

I've had a love/hate relationship with squirrels, mostly towards dislike in the love/hate spectrum ever since I watched a squirrel stick its head into a song thrush's nest and rummage around. This happened over a decade ago. The song thrush nest was immediately abandoned and my aversion to squirrels established.

Squirrel redemption came only recently when I watched a pair of squirrels feast on Norway maple tree seeds which were scattered all over the front grass. The seeds of the Norway maple tree, at least those from the one next door, have a propensity to germinate very successfully and, if you don't pull up the seedlings in their first or second year, they can be quite difficult to remove from the ground without recourse to a digging tool. Two squirrels combed the front grass for about half an hour picking up the helicopter seeds in their little front paws and eating the seed at the end of each flight blade. I still have not forgiven grey squirrels for one of their kind causing the abandonment of the song thrush nest.

January 12th

There is colour all over the Grange, especially in south-facing gardens. Rhododendrons, phygelius, ceanothus and more have got confused. These may be early spring flowers but this is still January. I was on the wander again up and down the streets in the Grange seeing what could catch my interest. There is a super, big *Pinus nigra*, a Black Pine, on the opposite side of Dick Place from the Deodar cedar that I like, but in the past I'd spent so long admiring the Deodar that I hadn't noticed the pine tree.

This pine has four-inch-long needles, in clusters of two: the clusters are called fascicles. This derives from the Latin, 'fascis', for 'bundle' or 'band'; the root also gives us 'fascia', which describes a band of tissue below the skin, and fasciitis, the ailment when this tissue gets inflamed. You may have suffered from plantar fasciitis, the most common cause of heel pain. The plantar fascia is the flat band of ligament which connects your heel bone to your toes and supports the arch of your foot. The word 'fascist' has the same derivation through the Italian 'fascio' for a political group, to which 'fascista', the fascists, belonged.

Walking through the Grange, I was heading for Morningside, another effete Edinburgh area, characterised in decades past as 'all fur coat and no knickers'. This was from a time when guests to Morningside establishments were greeted with, 'You'll have had your tea?' I was on a mission to deliver a borrowed DVD to Derek, a Cloisters regular. Derek cannot be a traditional Morningsider; he offered me tea.

On the walk home, I decided to say hello to a few of The Top Twenty trees in the Grange, as identified by Alistair Scott in the booklet,

'Trees in the Grange' (see December 7th). I visited a Walnut tree on Dick Place, an Atlas Cedar on Grange Loan, a Silver Willow on Lauder Road and a Paper-bark Birch in Dalrymple Crescent. From the names of these streets you should not be surprised to learn that in 1825, it was Sir Thomas Dick Lauder who made land from the Grange Estate available for development. This resulted in a series of parallel streets between two major roads, Grange Road to the north and Dick Place to the south, to form part of the Grange as it exists today.

There is harmony to the Grange because its houses, walls and streets were planned and constructed as an entity under rigorous conditions, and that harmony is maintained today through tight conservation regulations. The Grange Association (gaedin.co.uk) is vigilant in its monitoring of the area and it should be lauded for its effort and exactitude in ensuring that these regulations and laws are respected.

In all aspects of ownership, whether it be of houses, gardens, walls, trees, art, nature or any other article or aspect of value, we are firstly stewards, not owners. Stewardship is that duty of supervising and caring for something, so that no damage comes to it while it is in our custody, care or under our supervision. It is incumbent upon owners to follow the rule, 'First, do no harm', when intervention or change is considered. Change can and sometimes must occur, but let it happen with sensitivity and deliberation.

Printed in Great Britain
by Amazon